Scripture

Scripture

Nourished by the Word

Catholic Basics
A Pastoral Ministry Series

Margaret Nutting Ralph, Ph.D.

Thomas P. Walters, Ph.D.
Series Editor

NATIONAL CONFERENCE FOR
CATECHETAL LEADERSHIP

LOYOLAPRESS.
3441 N. ASHLAND AVENUE
CHICAGO, ILLINOIS 60657

NIHIL OBSTAT: Rev. Daniel J. Mahan, S.T.B., S.T.L.
Censor Librorum

IMPRIMATUR: Rev. Msgr. Joseph F. Schaedel
Vicar General/Moderator of the Curia

Given at Indianapolis, Indiana, on February 19, 2001

The *nihil obstat* and *imprimatur* are official declarations that a book is free of doctrinal and moral error. No implication is contained herein that those who have granted the *nihil obstat* and *imprimatur* agree with the content, opinions, or statements expressed.

Publisher's note: Some of the concepts included in this introductory book have already been published by Paulist Press. This book is written for NCCL with the cooperation and permission of Paulist Press.

Acknowledgments appearing on page 126 constitute a continuation of the copyright page.

Cover Design: Other Brother Design
Cover Illustration: Steve Snodgrass
Interior Illustrations: Other Brother Design

ISBN: 0-8294-1720-6

Published by Loyola Press, 3441 N. Ashland Avenue,
Chicago, Illinois 60657 U.S.A.
© 2002 The National Conference for Catechetical Leadership.

06 07 08 09 Bang 9 8 7 6 5

Table of Contents

About the Series   vii

Certification Standards:
    National Resources for Church Ministry   viii

Introduction   x

Chapter 1: What Is a Bible?   1

How Did the Bible Come into Existence?   2

Oral Tradition   7

Written Tradition   11

What Is Inspiration?   16

What Is Revelation?   17

For Reflection   18

Chapter 2: The Catholic Approach to Scripture   19

The Literary Form   20

The Beliefs of the Time   23

The Process of Revelation   25

Contextualists and Fundamentalists   27

A Look Back and a Look Forward   36

For Reflection   38

Chapter 3: Covenant Love   39

Covenant Love at the Time of Abraham and Beyond   40

Covenant Love at the Time of Moses and Beyond   45

Covenant Love at the Time of David and Beyond   47

Covenant Love at the Time of the Prophet Hosea and Beyond   48

Covenant Love at the Time of the Babylonian
    Exile and Beyond   51

Post-Babylonian Exile Insights Regarding Covenant Love   53

The Old Covenant and the New   58

For Reflection   59

CHAPTER 4: **THE KINGDOM OF GOD**   60

Understanding "Kingdom"   62

What Is a Parable?   64

When Will the Kingdom Come?   67

How Will We Recognize the Coming of the Kingdom?   71

Paradoxes About the Kingdom   73

The Return of the Son of Man   73

The Kingdom in the Gospel According to John   75

For Reflection   78

CHAPTER 5: **WHO IS JESUS CHRIST?**   79

Christology in the Gospel According to Mark   81

Christology in the Gospels According to Matthew and Luke   86

Christology in the Gospel According to John   95

A Look Back and a Look Forward   102

For Reflection   102

CHAPTER 6: **THE BIBLE IN THE LIFE OF THE CHURCH**   103

Scripture in Our Eucharistic Liturgy   105

Scripture in the Development of Church Doctrine   112

Scripture in Moral Decision Making   117

Scripture in Our Communal Prayer Life   120

Scripture in Personal Discernment   120

For Reflection   123

Abbreviations   124

Bibliography   125

Acknowledgments   126

About the Author   127

About the Series

Catholic Basics: A Pastoral Ministry Series offers an in-depth yet accessible understanding of the fundamentals of the Catholic faith for adults, both those preparing for lay ministry and those interested in the topics for their own personal growth. The series helps readers explore the Catholic tradition and apply what they have learned to their lives and ministry situations. Each title offers a reliable introduction to a specific topic and provides a foundational understanding of the concepts.

Each book in the series presents a Catholic understanding of its topic as found in Scripture and the teachings of the Church. Each of the authors has paid special attention to the documents of the Second Vatican Council and the *Catechism of the Catholic Church*, so that further learning can be guided by these core resources.

Chapters conclude with study questions that may be used for small group review or for individual reflection. Additionally, suggestions for further reading offer dependable guides for extra study.

The initiative of the National Conference of Catechetical Leadership led to the development of an earlier version of this series. The indispensable contribution of the series editor, Dr. Thomas Walters, helped ensure that the concepts and ideas presented here are easily accessible to a wide audience.

Certification Standards: National Resources for Church Ministry

Each book in this theology series relates to standards for theological competency identified in the resources listed below. Three national church ministry organizations provide standards for certification programs that serve their respective ministries. The standards were developed in collaboration with the United States Catholic Conference Commission on Certification and Accreditation. The fourth resource is the latest document, and it was developed to identify common goals of the three sets of standards.

Competency Based Certification Standards for Pastoral Ministers, Pastoral Associates and Parish Life Coordinators. Chicago: National Association for Lay Ministry, Inc. (NALM), 1994.

These standards address three roles found in pastoral ministry settings in the United States. The standards were the earliest to receive approval from the United States Catholic Conference Commission on Certification and Accreditation. Copies of the standards are available from the National Association for Lay Ministry, 5420 S. Cornell, Chicago, IL 60615-5604.

National Certification Standards for Professional Parish Directors of Religious Education. Washington, DC: National Conference for Catechetical Leadership, 1998.

The National Conference for Catechetical Leadership (NCCL) developed standards to foster appropriate initial education and formation, as well as continuing personal and professional development, of those who serve as Directors of Religious Education (DREs). The standards address various areas of knowledge and the abilities needed in the personal, theological, and professional aspects of the ministry. Also included is a code of ethics for professional catechetical leaders. Available from the National Conference for Catechetical Leadership, 3021 Fourth Street NE, Washington, DC 20017-1102.

NFCYM Competency-Based Standards for the Coordinator of Youth Ministry. Washington, DC: National Federation for Catholic Youth Ministry, 1996.

This document lays out the wide range of knowledge and skills that support ministry with young people as well as the successful leadership and organization of youth ministry wherever it may be situated. The standards are available from the National Federation for Catholic Youth Ministry, 415 Michigan Avenue NE, Suite 40, Washington, DC 20017-1518.

Merkt, Joseph T., ed. *Common Formation Goals for Ministry.* A joint publication of NALM, NFCYM, and NCCL, 2000.

Rev. Joseph Merkt compared the documentation of standards cited by three national organizations serving pastoral, youth, and catechetical ministries. The resulting statement of common goals identifies common ground for those who prepare persons for ministry as well as for the many people who wear multiple hats. Copies are available from NALM, NCCL, or NFCYM.

Introduction

You are probably familiar with a book titled *All I Really Need to Know I Learned in Kindergarten* by Robert Fulghum. That title would be far from the truth had the book in question been about Scripture. A book about Scripture might better be titled *Nearly Everything I Need to Know I Learned as an Adult.*

True, children can understand the plots of Bible stories, but in Bible stories the revelation is nearly always deeper than the plot. It is also true that children are capable of a deep spirituality and of understanding the core message of Scripture: God loves and saves. Nevertheless, to understand the concerns of biblical authors, to probe with them the mysteries of life and God's interaction with God's people, one must be an adult.

The fact that the Bible can be truly understood only by adults places a particular responsibility on us as adult Catholics. As you know, until the Second Vatican Council, Catholics were not encouraged to read the Bible. Nor was there an emphasis on adult religious education. As a result, most adult Roman Catholics do not know how to read the Bible, nor do they know what the Catholic Church teaches about how to understand the revelation that Scripture contains.

This book is written to help you help the Church overcome this problem, in relation both to yourself and to others. The book contains the basic and preliminary information that you and your fellow adult Catholics need to know to correctly understand Scripture. We all know from history, and perhaps from our personal experience, that some people use the Bible to instill hate and fear rather than love and peace. A person who misunderstands the Bible can be misguided as well as dangerous. It is important that we, as adults, understand the mistakes in thinking that result in these harmful interpretations so that we can name them for others. This book will help you do that.

There is no single volume on the face of the earth that contains more truth, wisdom, beauty, inspiration, and personal guidance than Scripture. There is no greater privilege we have than to make the revelation in Scripture available to others. But first, we have to understand it ourselves. This book has been written to help you understand, love, live by, and teach Scripture. It will help you understand:

- the meaning of inspiration, historical development, and literary criticism;

- the primary themes and basic concepts in Scripture, including covenant, kingdom, creation, salvation, and conversion;

- the scriptural foundations for Catholic moral teaching, conscience formation, and decision making;

- the use of Scripture in theological reflection;

- God's revelation in Creation, the person of Jesus, and lived experience;

- Christology, especially Jesus' life, mission, death, and Resurrection.

CHAPTER 1

What Is a Bible?

A partial answer to the question What is a Bible? is "A Bible is a collection of books—a library—of different kinds of writing or different literary forms." In order to begin to understand the library that we call the Bible, we need to have some background information about it. This background information may be more important for those of us who were raised in a Christian community and are familiar with the lectionary (the book that contains the three-year cycle of readings that we use at Mass) than it is for a person who starts to read a Bible with no presuppositions about it at all.

Christians who have been taught that God is the author of the Bible might never have asked themselves questions like How did God do it? Did God dictate the Bible to individual people? How did the Bible come into existence? Christians who hear the Old Testament read in the context of a Christian liturgy might never have wondered, What would a person who lived before Christ have understood this reading to be saying? Christians who, as children, heard stories about a man and a woman in a garden talking to God and a snake might never have asked themselves, What kind of writing is this story? Is it history? They might think, After all, God can do anything. God could make a snake talk if he wanted to.

In other words, Christians who heard lectionary readings as children, and who never studied the Bible as adults, might well have suspended their common sense. They might still be naively failing to ask the questions and seek out the answers that would allow them to truly appreciate the Bible. An adult who picked up a Bible with no background at all would certainly ask these questions. A first reading of the text would raise such questions in the mind of a reasonable person.

How Did the Bible Come into Existence?

The Bible as we now have it is the end product of a five-step process that took about two thousand years. The five steps of the process are events, oral tradition, written tradition, editing, and becoming canonical. We will explore each of these steps in detail.

EVENTS

God revealed himself to his people not through dictation but through events—events that occurred in the midst of the community. The events that underlie Scripture happened over a period of two thousand years, roughly from 1850 B.C. through the end of the first century A.D. The first historical person in this series of events was Abraham. God called Abraham and directed him to leave his homeland to set out for a land that God would show him. The earliest events of salvation history occurred in the lives of four generations of Abraham's family, named for the four patriarchs: Abraham, Isaac, Jacob, and Joseph. The stories of salvation history involving the patriarchs are in the Book of Genesis.

When we move from the Book of Genesis, the first book in the Bible, to the Book of Exodus, the second book, we jump forward four hundred years, to the time of Moses and the Exodus, thought to be about 1250 B.C. Although we know nothing of the intervening events, we do know that the promises made to Abraham formed the identity of the people and were passed on through the generations, because the call that Moses received was a call from the God of Abraham, Isaac, and Jacob.

The call directed Moses to lead his people out of slavery in Egypt and return to the land that God had promised Abraham. The many experiences of the Exodus—wandering in the desert, being fed with quail and manna, receiving the Law, and arriving in the Promised Land—were shared by the entire community. God revealed his saving power to everyone.

The next historic period is often referred to as the period of the judges. A judge was a charismatic leader called by God to rally the people to defeat a political enemy. During the period of the judges, which lasted some two hundred years, the people of Israel lived as tribes with no central political organization. When an enemy threatened, God would call forth a judge who would rally the tribes. Not until threatened by the Philistines did the Israelite tribes feel any need to be organized in a more centralized way.

The Philistines committed a great atrocity: They stole the ark of the Covenant, the most important symbol of God's presence with his people. The ark contained the Law that had been given to the people during their time in the desert. It symbolized their covenant relationship with God: They were God's Chosen People, and God would stay with them and protect them. For a Catholic, this would be comparable to someone stealing a tabernacle that contained consecrated hosts.

THE KINGDOM OF ISRAEL

Faced with the Philistines, many of the people began to insist, "We need a king like other nations!" Not everyone agreed, however, that the twelve tribes needed a king. After all, they already had a king. If they had a human king, would they begin to forget that God was their king? Thus began both the age of the kings and the age of the prophets. The kings provided a centralized and more powerful political organization; the prophets reminded the king and the nation that it was God who was really king.

Saul was the first king. If Saul were alive today, he undoubtedly would have benefited from therapy because he suffered terribly from jealousy. One of Saul's best soldiers, for example, was named David. He was the best friend of Saul's son and the husband of Saul's daughter. Although David's victories in battle were Saul's victories too, Saul became terribly jealous when he heard the people shout, "Saul has killed his thousands, and David his ten thousands" (1 Samuel 18:7). Saul, wounded in battle, finally fell on his own sword, and David became the next king.

David was the greatest king the nation ever had. He united the twelve tribes, defeated the Philistines, established his capital in Jerusalem, and brought the ark of the Covenant to Jerusalem, thus establishing Jerusalem as both the political and religious center of the nation. David did so much for his people's safety and well-being that he was seen as an expression of

God's promise to protect his people. He formed the ideas of the people regarding the kind of king God would send at other times of need: one like David.

David, however, was also a great sinner. He desired the wife of one of his soldiers, conceived a child with her, and then had her husband killed. The need for a prophet was obvious. David was acting as though he, not God, were king. Nathan, the prophet, spoke for God when he reprimanded the king and called him to conversion.

No other king was as great as David. David's son, Solomon, who succeeded David to the throne, erected many buildings in Jerusalem. Solomon completed the building of the Temple in Jerusalem. Solomon, however, also levied taxes. The tribes who lived in the north, because they did not benefit sufficiently from the buildings in Jerusalem, resented the taxes. As a result, the twelve tribes stayed united as a single nation for fewer than 100 years. In 922 B.C., the kingdom divided. The ten tribes in the north were called Israel; the two tribes in the south were called Judah.

For a number of years, until 721 B.C., both nations continued with their own respective kings and prophets. The role of the king as God's chosen leader was greatly emphasized in the south, where Jerusalem remained the capital. Still, the south had great prophets. The role of the prophet was greatly emphasized in the north, where the people had revolted against the king. Still, the north had kings. The two kingdoms coexisted until the Assyrians defeated the Northern Kingdom. The ten tribes in the north became the lost tribes of Israel. Their population intermarried with their conquerors and dropped out of the story of Old Testament events. Their story will continue, however, when we get to the New Testament and encounter the Samaritans. The Samaritans, considered unclean by the Jews, were the descendants of intermarriages between the Assyrians and the northern tribes.

The events underlying the Old Testament continue with the experiences of the Southern Kingdom for another two thousand years. In time, however, the last two tribes were also defeated, and thus began the second-most-traumatic time in the history of the people. Judah was defeated by the Babylonians in 587 B.C., and all the citizens of the upper class, including the king, were taken into exile in Babylon. The Babylonians also destroyed the Temple and devastated the land. The exiles asked themselves, Where is the God of covenant love who promised to protect us?

Some of the exiles returned to the Promised Land in 537 B.C., when Cyrus, who was a Persian, conquered the Babylonians. Cyrus was willing to let the Israelites go home. Not everyone who could return, however, wanted to return. Some exiles had made their way to Egypt. The Diaspora, the spreading of the people to other nations, had begun. Those who did return faced terrible hardships rebuilding their lives and their Temple. Never again were they able to achieve the greatness as a nation that they had enjoyed under David.

By 336 B.C., Alexander the Great was conquering that part of the world. He began the Hellenization of the area, that is, the beginning of the dominance of Greek culture. Except for a short period during the Maccabean revolt in 167 B.C., the Jews never again experienced freedom in the Promised Land. They lived under Greek rule until 63 B.C. and then under Roman rule. Jesus, as you know, was born during the Pax Romana, the time of peace under Roman rule.

The New Testament

The events that underlie the New Testament occurred, for the most part, in a single century. Jesus was born, lived in privacy until the last few years of his life, and then had a short public ministry that his followers as well as his enemies experienced as powerful in both word and deed.

Although Jesus was Jewish, his teachings were not accepted by the Jewish religious leaders of the day. Because they saw Jesus as a threat, the Pharisees and scribes, who were in positions of authority, wanted to silence Jesus. They lived under the authority of the Romans, however, so they could not inflict the death penalty. Jesus, therefore, was turned over to Roman authorities, who sentenced him to death. He was crucified, died, and was buried. After he was supposed to be dead, his followers claimed that he was still alive—that he had risen from the dead, had appeared to them, and had told them to await the coming of the Spirit. In the power of the Spirit, those who believed in Jesus carried on his ministry, powerful in both word and deed. The events that occurred during Jesus' lifetime and in the lifetime of his followers during that first century A.D. are the events that underlie the New Testament.

Oral Tradition

The second step in the process that resulted in the Bible as we now have it is oral tradition. None of the accounts that we have of biblical events are contemporary with the events themselves. We have no account, for example, of Abraham's experience from his own point of view. Contrary to the long-held belief that Moses wrote the first five books of the Bible, we have no accounts of Moses' experience from his own point of view. We have no accounts of Jesus' ministry from his point of view. All of the accounts of events were passed on by oral tradition, first within the community that initially experienced them, and then by later generations.

THE RELIABILITY OF ORAL TRADITION

The statement that our access to the events underlying the Old and New Testaments rests on oral tradition is upsetting for many people. They think of oral tradition as similar to gossip and so consider it unreliable. This is a misunderstanding. Oral tradition is, in fact, reliable, except in certain specific ways in which, because it does not claim reliability, we should not expect it.

Oral tradition is basically reliable because it is the product of the community. This is why oral tradition cannot be accurately compared to gossip or to the game called "telephone" that many of us played as children. When one person says something to another person in private, there is no one present to correct a mistake or a deliberate falsification. If the same misstatement was made in the hearing of the community, however, the community would correct it. Thus, the mistake, "Our Father, who art in heaven, Harold be thy name," has no chance of prevailing because a community that knows better will correct it.

The stories passed on by oral tradition faithfully represent the beliefs of the community. There are three ways, however, in which oral tradition does not claim accuracy. As we name and explain the ways in which we should not expect accuracy from oral tradition, we turn to the Gospels for examples. The concepts, however, are equally applicable to any literature that is the fruit of oral tradition.

First, no claim is made that oral tradition is passing on exact quotations. This failure to claim exact quotation, however, does not mean to say that there is no relationship between what we are reading in the Gospels and what Jesus actually said. To invest in a red-letter Bible—one that prints every word attributed to Jesus in red, as though Jesus' words bear more importance than all of the other words—is to feed a misunderstanding. Oral tradition passes on the sense of what was understood through the event.

When it comes to Jesus' ministry, a great deal of the meaning of Jesus' words was not understood until after the Resurrection. As those contemporaries of Jesus talked about their experiences, as they shared insights, and as they grew in understanding, they told stories about Jesus in such a way as to teach their listeners what they themselves had failed to understand at the time the events occurred. In other words, post-Resurrection insights are placed on Jesus' lips in the Gospels.

A second way in which oral tradition does not claim accuracy is that oral tradition does not always pass on the social setting in which an event occurred. That is why we sometimes read in two Gospels that Jesus said similar words but not to the same audience or in the same setting. This is easy to understand if we compare it to our own experience. One form of literature, for example, that is still passed on by oral tradition in our culture is the joke. When we hear and appreciate a joke, and then pass it on to someone we think will enjoy it as well, we do not pass on the social setting in which we heard the joke. We do not begin by saying, "Tom told me this joke last Friday while we were walking on Main Street." That information is irrelevant to the point. Just so, when those in the early Church retold Jesus' parables and sayings, they did not describe the setting in which Jesus first told the parable or the place where Jesus was standing at the time. The settings that are described in the Gospel are often important to note if we want to understand the full meaning of the Gospel, but we make a mistake if we assume that the settings are there for the purpose of historical accuracy.

In Matthew's Gospel, for example, Jesus is pictured as standing on a mountain when he teaches the Beatitudes. In Luke's Gospel, however, Jesus is pictured standing on a plain. Because Jesus' words were passed on through oral tradition, it is likely that neither Gospel editor knew exactly where Jesus was standing. Because Matthew pictured Jesus as the new Moses, with authority from God to promulgate a new Law, however, Matthew made a point of placing Jesus on the mountain. After all, Moses was on the mountain when he promulgated the first Law. Matthew provided the setting not for historical reasons but for theological reasons.

The third way in which oral tradition does not claim accuracy is in the historical chronology of events. When those in the early Church were collecting stories of Jesus' mighty acts, they did not care in what order the mighty acts occurred. What difference did it make whether the healing of the woman with the hemorrhage came before or after the healing of the man with the withered hand?

You will probably remember the story of Jesus cleansing the Temple of the money changers. At what point in Jesus' ministry did this happen? The Gospels do not give us access to the information we would need to answer such a question. We can see that in the Gospels of Matthew, Mark, and Luke, Jesus was pictured as cleansing the Temple late in his ministry, as he entered Jerusalem just before his Passion, death, and Resurrection. In John's Gospel, however, Jesus was pictured cleansing the Temple early in his ministry, right after the account of the wedding at Cana. So which was it? The answer to the question is both unavailable and irrelevant. The episode was placed in each Gospel at the point at which it appears for a reason, but the reason is theological, not historical. Oral tradition does not claim accuracy in historical chronology.

One other characteristic of literature that comes to us through oral tradition deserves to be noted. In oral tradition the storytellers and those listening to the stories have a great deal in common: They are contemporaries living in the same culture. Many things presumed to be known between them could be completely unknown to us today. For this reason, some background information to biblical stories is often helpful. It may be that the storyteller presumed that his audience knew something about which we are entirely unaware.

ORAL TRADITION RESULTS IN A LAYERED TEXT

Oral traditions about the events surrounding Jesus continued for a generation before the stories were written and edited in the form in which we now have them. This is a relatively short time. The stories about Abraham, for example, were passed on through oral tradition for six hundred years. No story about Abraham that we have today reached the form it is in until after the Exodus. The stories about Abraham and the other patriarchs are told in the light of the Exodus experience.

As stories were told, details were added that were contemporary with the storyteller rather than with the original setting of the story. This made the story more interesting and understandable for each succeeding generation. The earliest stories about Noah and the flood, for instance, obviously preceded the Exodus experience (1250 B.C.). Archeologists tell us that there was a flood in that part of the world that dates to about 3000 B.C., and a virtuous person named Noah is mentioned as a contemporary of the patriarchs (1850 B.C.). One of the directions that God is pictured as giving Noah involves clean and unclean animals. The rules about clean and unclean animals could not have been part of the original story because they were developed later in the history of the Chosen People. A later storyteller, however, incorporated this detail in order to make the story more understandable and enjoyable for his contemporary audience. The main point of the story did not change, but some of the details did. Thus stories passed on through oral tradition become layered, like an old tree. They reveal their life through many generations by the circle of details that grows up around their core.

Written Tradition

In time, various parts of the oral tradition began to be written down, but the fact that some things were written did not mean that the oral tradition ceased. In fact, the two continued side by side. As our example, we turn again to the New Testament, but the same concept is applicable to the Old Testament.

The earliest writing in the New Testament is not the Gospel of Matthew, which appears first. The earliest writing is Paul's First Letter to the Thessalonians. Paul went to Thessalonia and preached the Gospel. In other words, the Thessalonians first heard the Gospel through oral tradition. Then Paul moved on to teach elsewhere. After Paul was gone, and the newly converted Thessalonians learned to live the Gospel and looked forward to the Second Coming, they experienced a crisis: Some of the believers died. The rest of the community then had a question for Paul that Paul had not addressed while he was with them: Will believers who die before the Second Coming also be taken up to heaven with the risen Lord? Paul responded to their question, along with some other matters, in a letter. So the Thessalonians had both an oral and a written tradition.

Over time, various parts of the oral tradition were written down, but always in order to serve a contemporary audience. The written tradition did not take form because someone said, "Two thousand years from now people are going to want to know about this." Rather, the written tradition, like the oral tradition, was aimed at a contemporary audience and attempted to address the questions and needs of that audience.

EDITING

At various times in the course of events that are at the core of both the Old and New Testaments, editors went over the inherited oral and written traditions of the people and arranged them into a connected narrative. The earliest editing of the first five books of the Old Testament is believed to have taken place after the Exodus, perhaps during the time when David had established a degree of peace and security in the Holy Land (1000 B.C.).

Imagine that you were alive during the time of King David. Imagine also that you had heard the stories of the patriarchs and of God's mighty acts of salvation during the time of the Exodus. Now, after two hundred difficult years of settling Canaan, here you are living in the Promised Land with a great king. Wouldn't you feel that all of the hopes and dreams of your ancestors had finally come true? In the light of this belief, all the oral and written traditions were gathered and arranged to tell a connected story.

Now imagine that you are living in the Northern Kingdom after the kingdoms have divided. You obviously would not agree that all of God's promises were being fulfilled through the house of David, or you would not have rebelled against the house of David. You still embrace the story of the patriarchs, you are still in awe of God's saving power during the Exodus, and you still regard yourself as involved in a relationship of covenant love with God, as God's Chosen People. In the light of recent events, however, you have a different point of view about past events. One can see how the light of experience and new insights caused the stories to be retold and edited from a different point of view.

Now imagine that you are living in the Southern Kingdom after the Northern Kingdom has fallen. You have been so loyal to the house of David as an expression of covenant love that the Exodus experience and the Law have faded from your mind and practice. You have been traumatized by the fall of the Northern Kingdom. Surely those in the Northern Kingdom must have displeased God to have come to such an unhappy end. What might you learn from their experience? This kind of thinking led to a period of reform in the Southern Kingdom (622 B.C.) and a further editing of the inherited oral and written traditions of the people.

Finally, imagine that you are living after the Babylonian exile (587–537 B.C.). You and your people have just been through the most disillusioning experience possible. Everything you believed in has been destroyed: king, kingdom, and Temple. Why had God let his people suffer so terribly? Then, as events unfold in such a way that you are able to return home, you find that the person God sent to save you is not even a Jew. You have been saved by Cyrus, a Persian! Could a Persian be an instrument of God's saving power? It seems so, but what a mystery! In the light of all these mysterious events, the story was edited once more and retold in the light of newly gained insights.

In going over the inherited traditions, if the editors found stories that did not entirely agree with each other, they did not choose between them; rather, they included them both. That is why, for example, we find more than one account of events and accounts of events from different points of view in the Old Testament. The editors respected the insights of each generation, including their own.

The Gospels of Matthew, Mark, and Luke are three separate examples of edited accounts of oral and written traditions about the events surrounding Jesus' life, death, and Resurrection. In fact, Luke described the whole process as he began his Gospel.

> *Since many have undertaken to set down an order-*
> *ly account of the events that have been fulfilled*
> *among us, just as they were handed on to us by*
> *those who from the beginning were eyewitnesses*
> *and servants of the Word, I too decided, after inves-*
> *tigating everything carefully from the very first, to*
> *write an orderly account for you, most excellent*

Theophilus, so that you may know the truth concerning the things about which you have been instructed.

(Luke 1:1–4)

Luke did not claim to be an eyewitness; rather, he explained that he was the editor of inherited oral and written traditions about events.

The arrangement of books in the Old and New Testaments is one more result of editing. The books do not appear in the order in which they were written but in an edited order. The Hebrew canon includes thirty-nine books divided into three categories: the Law, the Prophets, and the Writings. The Law, or Pentateuch, includes the first five books of the Bible *(Genesis, Exodus, Leviticus, Numbers, and Deuteronomy)*. These books are about the origin of the nations. The Prophets includes both the books of the older prophets *(Joshua, Judges, 1 and 2 Samuel, 1 and 2 Kings)* and the later prophets *(Isaiah, Jeremiah, Ezekiel, Hosea, Joel, Amos, Obadiah, Jonah, Micah, Nahum, Habakkuk, Zephaniah, Haggai, Zechariah, and Malachi)*. These books are about the constant call to be faithful to the covenant relationship during the years of settling and living in the Holy Land. The Writings include the Psalms, Proverbs, Job, Song of Songs, Ruth, Lamentations, Ecclesiastes, Esther, Daniel, Ezra, Nehemiah, and 1 and 2 Chronicles. The Writings are about the reinterpretations and new understandings that became necessary after the horrendous experience of the Babylonian exile. Catholics also recognize seven additional books: Tobit, Judith, 1 and 2 Maccabees, Wisdom, Ecclesiasticus, and Baruch. In Catholic tradition, these books are included in the Writings. The reason for the inclusion of these books in the Catholic canon, and not in the canon of most Christian traditions, will be explained shortly. All Christians agree on the twenty-seven books included in the New Testament.

BECOMING CANONICAL

Not every written work that is the fruit of oral and written traditions about the events that underlie Scripture appears in the table of contents of your Bible. Those that are included are called "canonical"; those that are excluded are called "apocryphal." The word *canon* means "ruler." Thus books that are canonical are those that have been accepted by generations of the believing community as faithfully passing on the truth about their experiences and beliefs, and as being spiritually nourishing. In other words, they are the books by which the community's faith and beliefs are measured.

The canon was established not by hierarchical mandate but by the movement of the Spirit in the whole community. Let us use the New Testament as our example. During the second century other gospels circulated, other than the four that we now have. These gospels were not condemned and burned. If you choose, you can read the gospel of Thomas or the gospel of Jude today. The believing community, however, preferred some gospels to others. As the early Church leaders compared notes about what was becoming accepted and beloved, the four Gospels that we now have continued to be used more and more, while others fell into disuse. By the end of the second century, the Gospel canon was established. By the end of the fourth century, the whole New Testament canon was established.

While both the Old and the New Testament canons were established by the believing communities, both were pronounced "closed" by the voice of authority. The Old Testament canon was closed at the Council of Jamnia, in the first century, by those in leadership in the Jewish religion. Their decision was a reaction to the growth of literature surrounding Jesus Christ. Many Jews who believed in Christ were acting as though the literature that grew up around Jesus was appropriate for inclusion in Scripture. Jews who did not believe in Christ would obviously find this objectionable.

Not all Jews of the time, however, had the same canon. After the Diaspora, and after the Hellenization of that part of the world, the Old Testament had been translated into Greek. This Greek translation was called the Septuagint. In the several hundred years preceding Christ, some Greek books were added to the Septuagint that were not included in the original Old Testament. Because they were not in the Old Testament, they were not included in the Hebrew canon that was closed at the Council of Jamnia. They remained, however, in the Septuagint, which was the translation that St. Jerome used when he translated the Old Testament into Latin. Jerome's translation, the Vulgate, has remained through history as a source for Catholic translations. Translators during the Reformation preferred to limit themselves only to Hebrew texts, and so did not include the late additions to the Septuagint. It is these books to which we were referring earlier when we said that seven books included in the Catholic canon are not in the canon of most other Christian traditions.

The New Testament canon was declared closed at the Council of Trent (1545–1563). Again, the action was a defensive one. It was taken not because there was a move to add unwanted books to the canon but because there was a move to eliminate some books that had been accepted through the centuries. The Council of Trent declared authoritatively that the New Testament canon would remain as it had been.

What Is Inspiration?

Now that we know how the Bible came into existence, we are better able to respond to the questions, What do we mean when we say that God is the author of the Bible? and What do we mean by the word *inspiration*? Obviously, when we claim that God is the author of the Bible, we don't mean that God put pen to paper, or quill to scroll, and wrote the Bible. Nor when we use the word *inspiration* do we mean that God dictated the text to one inspired author. Certainly we do claim that those who wrote sections of the Bible were inspired, but the word *inspiration* is applicable on a much broader basis. We claim that inspiration— God's help in perceiving and understanding—occurred at every step of the process that resulted in the Bible.

First, the original generations that experienced the events of their daily lives as events in which God was powerful and present, as events through which God was revealing himself to the community, were inspired. Next, those in the community who were able to interpret the events religiously and pass on that interpretation in a convincing manner to their contemporaries through oral tradition were inspired. The storytellers of every generation who fed the faith of their contemporaries through their stories were inspired. Those who began to write down the stories were inspired. Those who edited the inherited traditions in the light of subsequent events were inspired. Those of every generation who found themselves longing to hear of their God, and who found that longing satisfied in the inspired stories of their ancestors and their contemporaries, were inspired. These are the people who received the Word and were instrumental in its becoming canonical.

Finally, we might also think of ourselves as inspired. It is only through the indwelling of the Spirit within us that we long to read, understand, and teach Scripture. It is only through the indwelling of the Spirit that we long to understand the revelation that Scripture contains.

What Is Revelation?

What are we claiming when we say that the Bible contains "revelation"? We are claiming that what the Bible teaches us about God, about our relationship with God, and about what God would have us do to build up his kingdom rather than tear it down is true. We are claiming that what we need to know in order to cooperate with God's saving grace is contained in the Bible. In order to understand the revelation that Scripture contains, however, we need to know how to read the Bible. The approach that the Catholic Church teaches to help us understand the revelation that Scripture contains is explained in our next chapter.

❧✝❧

For Reflection

1. Has God revealed himself to you through events? Explain.

2. Have you found that you understand God's role in events better in hindsight than you did as the events occurred? Does this affect the way you tell the story of the events? Explain.

3. Has reading this chapter caused you to revise your previous understanding of *inspiration* and *revelation*? If so, how? How would you explain the meaning of *inspiration* and *revelation*?

CHAPTER 2

The Catholic Approach to Scripture

D o you think of a terrorist suicide bomber as a religious martyr or as a murderer? You are undoubtedly aware that many evil acts are done in the name of religion, and Scripture is often quoted as justification for carrying out these acts. How would you respond to a person who defends a terrorist bombing in this way: "Didn't God say, 'and when the Lord your God gives them [other nations] over to you and you defeat them, then you must utterly destroy them. Make no covenant with them and show them no mercy' (Deuteronomy 7:2)? Didn't God say, 'No one has greater love than this, to lay down one's life for one's friends' (John 15:13)? That's what a terrorist bomber is doing."

It is obvious from this example that if we take sentences of the Bible out of context, attribute them to God, and then picture God saying the words directly to us, we can easily misinterpret their meaning. That is why the Roman Catholic Church teaches us to be *contextualists* when we read Scripture, that is, to read Scripture passages *in context*. The first Church document that taught us to be contextualists was *Divino Afflante Spiritu*, published in 1943. The teachings of this document were reaffirmed and expanded upon in the Second Vatican Council document titled *The Dogmatic Constitution on Divine Revelation* (*Dei Verbum* [*DV*], 1965) and reaffirmed again in the *Catechism of the Catholic Church* ([*CCC*], see #110, 112, 120, 126).

There are basically three contexts to be considered if we want to correctly understand the revelation that Scripture contains. These contexts are the literary form, the beliefs of the time, and the process of revelation that takes place within Scripture.

The Literary Form

As we mentioned in the first chapter, the Bible is not a book with chapters but a library with books. This is an extremely important distinction, and one that many people seem to ignore. If the

Bible were a book with chapters, and we correctly understood the kind of writing it is, then we could keep a single frame of mind, a single set of expectations. We could read it from beginning to end without misunderstanding any of it. However, because the Bible is a library of books of different kinds of writing, we must revise our frame of mind, our expectations, as we move from one literary form to another. If we fail to do this, we fail to understand what we are reading.

Some people are resistant to the idea that the Bible is a library of books of different literary forms. They argue that because the Bible contains a great deal of oral literature that was passed on around campfires from generation to generation, we shouldn't need a degree in literature to be able to understand it. Those who propose this argument are correct. The Bible is a collection of popular literature intended to be understood by the proverbial "person in the street." The difficulty, however, is not with people's ability to understand a variety of literary forms, but with their realizing that this ability needs to be brought to bear on the Bible. People need to be given permission to bring to their reading of the Bible the same common sense that they bring to their reading of everything else, including a newspaper.

As an example, soon after Princess Diana died in an automobile accident, I read three different articles dealing with the tragedy, each in a different literary form. The first was a front-page story that discussed the blood-alcohol level of the driver, the speed of the car, and the possible role of the paparazzi. The second article contained the lyrics of the song that Elton John sang at the funeral, in which Diana was eulogized as "our English rose." The third was a "Doonesbury" strip, in which Zonker had been hired by the royal family as a consultant to help them bring out their "common" side. Zonker was pictured greeting the royal family with the words, "Hi, Liz! Hi, Chuck! How ya doin'?"

Although all three of these articles were in the newspaper, rooted in an event, and grappling with the truth, they were very different literary forms. Only the first article responded to the question, What happened? The function of the second article, the song, was not to answer the question, What happened? but to express the love and admiration of an adoring public. Eulogies, by form and function, leave some things out. The third literary form, although it contained a fictional character and fictional dialogue, was still related to the historic event, and still taught something true about the significance of that event in the lives of the people. Had I read the second and third articles with the same frame of mind with which I read the first, I would have completely misinformed myself. When we misunderstand a literary form, we misunderstand the intent of the author. When we misunderstand a literary form when we read the Bible, we misunderstand the revelation.

Any literary form is an appropriate vehicle for revelation. Writing that responds to the question, What happened? is certainly a possibility, but so is every other kind of writing: myth, legend, parable, allegory, fiction, debate, apocalyptic writing. Each of these kinds of writing is distinct, and each can easily be misunderstood if it is mistaken for something other than what it is. In order to understand any book in the Bible, we must correctly understand its literary form.

An example from the Bible will illustrate how dangerous it is to fail to ask the question, What literary form am I reading? One inspired biblical author chose debate as his literary form. If you are the author of a debate, you are the author of the side of the argument with which you agree, as well as the side of the argument with which you disagree. The author of this particular debate lived at a time when people believed that all suffering was due to sin, but this inspired person did not believe this. He believed that an innocent person could suffer and that this suffering had some purpose in God's provident plan. He also believed, however, that to attribute all the suffering that is observable to a God who punishes is to misrepresent God. It presents God as less loving than he actually is.

In order to challenge the beliefs of his time, the inspired author wrote a book in which he pictured the sufferings of an innocent person: Job. He then pictured Job's friends trying to figure out the reason for Job's suffering. The friends, unlike the reading audience, did not know that Job was innocent. They debated the issue and arrived at the conclusion that Job must have sinned or he would not be suffering. Then God appeared. It is through what God said, not through what Job's friends said, that the author presented the truth he was teaching: Not all suffering was due to sin.

Now, imagine that you are at Mass. The lector gets up and reads a selection from the Book of Job. At the end of the reading, the lector says, "The Word of the Lord," and you respond, "Thanks be to God." What the lector read, however, is a passage from the Book of Job that was on the lips of Eliphaz, one of Job's friends who misunderstood the truth. So if you think of God as having spoken the words that were on Eliphaz's lips, you are putting God's authority behind the very idea against which the author wrote. You have not merely misunderstood what the inspired author was teaching, but you have taken as true the very idea that the author was teaching as false.

This illustrates a point that we mentioned in the Introduction: An acquaintance with the lectionary is not an acquaintance with the Bible. We discussed the relationship between the two in the last chapter. In the meantime, let it suffice to say that the Lectionary takes passages out of the context in which they appear in the Bible and places them in a different context. Can you think of any book on the face of the earth that you would expect to understand if you read random chapters in random order once a week? In order to understand any book of the Bible, you must read it.

The Beliefs of the Time

The second context that must be considered if we want to understand the revelation that the Bible contains is the context of the beliefs of the people who lived at the time the book was written. Sometimes, in the course of teaching a universal truth, an inspired author will say something by way of application or elaboration that is not essential to the truth being taught but that makes that truth more understandable to the contemporary audience. If a later generation discovers that something said in the application or elaboration is not scientifically accurate, but instead represents a presumption of the time, does that mean that the author was not inspired? Does it mean that the book does not contain revelation? The answer to each of these questions is no.

When we say that an author was inspired, we claim that the author had spiritual insight: What the author taught about God and our relationship with God was true. We do not claim that the author had God's point of view. We do not claim that the author had knowledge on subjects not related to his topic that no one else in his generation had. An inspired author who lived in 450 B.C., and who realized that a loving God created all that exists, did not also realize that the earth is round instead of flat. The inspired author, like everyone else in his generation, presumed that the earth was flat. So when he pictured God making the earth, he pictured God making it flat. His purpose was not to teach the shape of the earth but to teach the relationship between God and the created order.

Again, an example from our world will make the point clear. Imagine that you are a hopeful lover out in a boat on a starry night. You say to your beloved, "As long as the sun rises in the east and sets in the west, I will love you." Your beloved responds, "You know, the sun doesn't actually rise and set. You see, the earth is round, and it is turning in relation to the sun, and that's what makes it appear to us that the sun is rising and setting. Since your statement is scientifically inaccurate, I conclude that you do not love me." Would you consider this a successful interchange? Through history, God has had this kind of problem with his beloved: us.

When a person fails to distinguish between the core universal truth that an author taught, and various presumptions and applications that the author had also included—and so puts the authority of Scripture behind the presumption or application—

that person sometimes ends up persecuting someone in God's name. Historically, this has been the case in regard to Galileo and evolutionists, to name only two examples. We get into dangerous territory when we use passages from Scripture to prove that our point of view is correct if the question we are addressing is not the same question that the inspired author was addressing. We discuss this topic further, and with more examples, in the last chapter, when we discuss the role of Scripture in moral decision making.

The Process of Revelation

The third context that we need to consider if we want to understand the revelation that Scripture contains is the two-thousand-year process of arriving at the knowledge that is revealed in the Bible. This is an important context for everyone to consider, but especially for those of us who received our early education through a catechism format. In a catechism format, we memorized answers to questions—answers that did not contradict one another. We were never asked if we agreed with the answers. Although the answers gave us extremely valuable information, and a vocabulary with which to name and talk about the spiritual realm, they did not help us realize that we were probing mysteries beyond our abilities to understand or that the best of all our answers was still inadequate to the truth.

The Bible, on the other hand, probes mystery. The Bible reveals a two-thousand-year process of people reflecting on their experience and on the significance of their experience in the context of their relationship with God. As the years passed, their insights increased. Early insights, however, were not shown to be completely wrong. Rather, those ideas that originally may have been understood to be the whole truth were later understood to be partial insights, steps on the road to a fuller understanding of the truth.

Modern-day readers who do not realize that the Bible reveals a process of revelation are prone to make two serious mistakes.

One mistake is to decide that the Bible contradicts itself and so cannot be revelation. The other is to mistake an early insight for the fullness of truth and so to attribute to the Bible a less-developed revelation than the Bible actually contains.

I recently heard a discussion on television that illustrated these mistakes. Two men, each ordained and representing a Christian tradition, were discussing the morality of the death penalty. One was in favor of it; the other was not. Each man supported his point of view by appealing to the authority of Scripture. The person who was in favor of the death penalty added authority to his words by quoting Exodus: "If any harm follows, then you shall give life for life, eye for eye, tooth for tooth, hand for hand, foot for foot, burn for burn, wound for wound, stripe for stripe" (21:23). The second claimed that the passage in Exodus should be dismissed because Jesus said, "You have heard that it was said, 'An eye for an eye and a tooth for a tooth.' But I say to you, do not resist an evildoer. But if anyone strikes you on the right cheek, turn the other also" (Matthew 5:38–39).

Christians listening to this debate might be puzzled. Some might conclude, "Since the Bible contradicts itself on this question, the Bible can't be revelation." Others might conclude, "The New Testament is revelation, but the Old Testament is not." Still others might decide, "Since the Bible doesn't answer this question directly, the Bible has nothing to offer in trying to reach a solution." All of these conclusions would be wrong.

If we understand that the Bible reflects a process of coming to knowledge, a process of revelation, we see that the statement "a life for a life" was not a mistake but an early insight, a partial truth. This passage in Exodus teaches against revenge. It is saying that we cannot, in anger, do worse to someone who has hurt us than they have done to us: "An eye for an eye and a tooth for a tooth." This teaching is a great step forward in understanding the ramifications of the fact that God loves each of us, and so we must learn to love one another. Jesus did not deny the truth of the insight of his ancestors; rather, he built on that insight. A loving God wants even more than our refraining to act toward one another in a vengeful manner. A loving God wants us to learn to forgive, just as God forgives us. That is why Jesus said that he did not come to destroy the Law and the prophets but to fulfill them. The two teachings—the admonition against revenge and the admonition to act lovingly, even toward a person who harms us—are not contradictions but steps in a process. Each contains revelation. To quote only the first is to fail to attribute to Scripture the fullness of revelation that Scripture contains.

Contextualists and Fundamentalists

We see, then, that the Catholic Church teaches us to consider context in order to determine meaning. We have named and explained three contexts that must be considered: the literary form, the beliefs of the time, and the process of revelation. When we consistently ask questions about context as part of our process of understanding Scripture, we act as contextualists. When we fail to consider context, we act as fundamentalists. This is the defining difference between the two. It's not that one considers the authors to be inspired and the other does not. It's not that one considers the books to contain revelation and the other does not. And it's not that one considers Scripture to be a living word that can form us and speak to the inner recesses of our hearts and the other does not. The difference is not that fundamentalists have more faith and contextualists have more brains. The only difference is whether or not a person considers context in order to determine meaning.

AN APPLICATION OF THE CONTEXTUALIST METHOD TO GENESIS 1–3

We use the contextualist method of interpretation when we consider the contexts of literary form, the beliefs of the time, and the process of revelation in order to understand the revelation that Scripture contains. It remains, then, to demonstrate the fruitfulness of this method by applying it to the Creation stories. In addition to applying what we have learned about context, we will be applying what we learned in the first chapter about how the Bible came into existence. Everything learned so far is necessary background information for all that follows.

The first step in the interpretation of any text of Scripture is to read the text. Try to read it with a fresh mind, as though you have never read or heard it before. Many people are absolutely positive that certain details are in a story in Scripture not because they have read the text but because they have heard the story line repeated in some rendition of Bible stories for children or seen the story depicted in pictures or movies. Others claim familiarity from lectionary readings. The lectionary, however, often leaves passages out, selecting only those verses that are appropriate for the liturgical setting. In order to have any knowledge of the Bible, it is necessary to read the Bible itself, to let the biblical text have the first word. Before proceeding further, read the first three chapters of the Book of Genesis.

Questions Raised by Reading the Text

If you picked up the Book of Genesis in a library without any previous knowledge about it and read the first three chapters, you would realize some important facts just from applying your common sense to the text. First, you would realize that the author or authors were not attempting to write history. History, by definition, involves accounts of events that were witnessed and about which we have either oral or written traditions. A story that begins before any human being was alive is not claiming to be history. In addition, the chapters include a serpent that can carry on a logical conversation with human beings. We all know from experience that snakes do not talk. This is obviously a literary device. The storyteller gives us a hint about the literary form of the story we are reading by using personification—by describing something that is not human as having human characteristics.

Next, you would realize that the author or authors were not teaching science. After all, a day is a day because of the amount of time it takes for the earth to rotate in relation to the sun. So for two days to have passed before the sun is created is impossible from a scientific point of view. Obviously, the questions a scientist would ask, and the questions that the first three chapters of Genesis address, are not the same.

You would also realize that you might well be reading the work of more than one person. One story is complete: God creates everything that exists and then rests on the seventh day. Then, after everything has been created, including male and female made in God's image, the story backs up and says that there are as yet no plants and no people to till the ground. Then a second story is told, one that actually contradicts some of the details in the first story. The first three chapters of Genesis contain two separate stories, one not a continuation of the other.

Genesis 1:1–2:4

Since the first three chapters of Genesis contain two separate stories, we deal with each story individually. The first story in Genesis is about the creation of all that exists. The time of the plot of the story—the origin of the earth—and the time of the author, however, are obviously not the same. The author was not claiming to be a witness of or a contemporary of the events that he described. We can tell by the structure of the story—a workweek—that the author lived at a time when his society was structured into six workdays and a Sabbath. Otherwise, the author would not have been able to structure his story in this way.

This observation often takes people by surprise. They bring with them a presumption that everything they read in the Bible is history. They also bring a presumption that because God wrote the Bible, the story was written from God's point of view. That is how the story can be about things that were not witnessed by human beings. They understand the details about the Sabbath as describing the origin of the Sabbath—God rested on the seventh day when he created the world—not as offering a hint about the society in which the author lived.

With what we have already learned about the origin of the Bible, however, and about the contextualist approach, we understand the error of these presumptions. Because God worked through human authors, and those human authors shared the knowledge and presumptions of their contemporaries on every subject but the one subject that they are addressing—their spiritual insights—a detail about a workweek is information about the time of the author. When Bill Cosby tells his story of Noah, in which a driveway, a newspaper, and a camera appear, we know that the author of this version of Noah lived at a time when driveways, newspapers, and cameras were part of the culture.

In fact, Scripture scholars believe that this first story in the Book of Genesis was placed in its present position, as a preface to all that follows, during the last editing of the first five books of the Old Testament. This priestly editing took place after the Babylonian exile, when the Israelites were rebuilding Jerusalem and re-establishing the beliefs of their ancestors. When put in this historical context, the teachings in the story become even clearer.

The story is most obviously about the author's insight that everything that exists is here because a loving God created it. A person who had no knowledge of the cultural setting of the author could find this truth in the story. A person who understood the beliefs to which the Israelites had been exposed while in Babylon, and how these beliefs conflicted with the traditions of the ancestors, would see additional teachings.

First, the ancestors had believed in one God, while the Babylonians believed in many gods. Among the gods of the Babylonians were the sun and the moon. In this story, the priests reaffirmed for the Israelites that there was just one God and that the sun and the moon were not gods but creations of God. The sun and the moon did not have power over human beings. Rather, the sun and the moon measured night and day.

The Israelites had a basic understanding of the goodness of all creation. The Babylonians, on the other hand, believed that spirit was good but matter was not. The author of the creation story emphasized the traditional belief in the goodness of all that God made. God specifically said at the end of each day that what had been created was good, and at the end of the sixth day, God said that all that had been created was *very* good.

Finally, among all of God's creation, the Israelites recognized themselves as beloved of God and, at the core, very good because they were made in God's own image. The Babylonians, however, thought of human beings as having been created not in the image of a loving God but from the corpse of a rebellious and defeated god. In the Babylonian creation story, human beings were made from defective matter, and so, at their core, were not good. The priestly editors reaffirmed for their people their own basic goodness and dignity.

It is not that the stories of our origins deny our experience of sin. As we will soon see, the second story in Genesis deals with this unwelcome truth, known from experience. The stories of our origin, however, do not start with sin. Rather, they start with the goodness of all creation, and particularly the goodness of the human race that, male and female, is made in God's own image.

Now that we understand the meaning of the story, we are in a better position to name the literary form of the story. The story of Creation is a story about reality but not a description of historical events. It deals with the reality that everything exists. The question is, How did everything that exists come into existence? The story also helps orient human beings in a moral universe; it helps us understand our place in relationship to God and the rest of creation. Because the topic at hand is, in a real sense, beyond anyone's experience or total understanding, the author had no choice but to address the topic through symbolic language.

An imaginative and symbolic story about a reality that is beyond our comprehension is, by definition, a myth. The word *myth* has to be used carefully because it is spelled and pronounced the same way as another word with an entirely different meaning. The word *myth* is used in English to describe something that was once believed to be true but is now known to be false. This is the meaning of the word in the title *Ten Myths About*

Old Age. This use of the word, however, has no relationship to the way in which we use the word: as the name of a literary form.

This distinction is important because many people, when they hear the word myth applied to a story in the Bible, think that it means this story was once believed to be true but is now known to be false. This is not what is being said at all, however. To use the word "myth" to name a literary form is not to comment on the truth or falsity of the myth any more than to call something a "letter" is to comment on the truth or falsity of its contents. That this Creation story is in the canon is testimony to the fact that generations of the faithful have believed that what it teaches is true.

Another problem many people encounter when they hear the Creation story referred to as a myth is that they think the whole Bible is being referred to as a myth. Such persons may well ask, If you are going to say the story about creation is a myth, what is keeping you from saying that the story of the Resurrection is a myth? These persons have forgotten that the Bible is a library of different literary forms. To define the form of one story is not to say anything at all about any story but the one being discussed.

A myth, as we have noted, has no claim to scientific accuracy. Scientific writing and myth have different functions. Scientific writing concerns itself with studying material forms and recurring phenomena. If we want to address the question of God's role in events, we cannot choose scientific writing as the form in which to address the subject. God is not a material form. We move out of the methodology of a scientist when we start to teach about God.

In addition, the author of the Creation story lived before the scientific age. He presumed that the earth was flat and that it had something like a dish over it. It is this "dish" to which the author referred when he talked about the water above the firmament and the water below the firmament. The author pictured God making the earth as the author presumed the earth to be. The fact that science has now shown us that these presumptions were in error is irrelevant to the point of the story.

Genesis 2:4–3:24

The second story in the Book of Genesis is often called the second story of creation. When we think about it, however, we realize that this is a misnomer. This story is not about Creation from beginning to end, as was the first story. Rather, Creation is merely an early plot element in the story. If we were to summarize the plot, Creation would not even be mentioned. Rather, this is a story about a man and a woman who lived in a place of no suffering. God told them not to eat from a tree of the knowledge of good and evil. They did eat of the forbidden tree, and they were no longer free from suffering.

As was true in the first story, the author dealt with a subject that was rooted in reality, in everyday experience: people suffer. If God is all-powerful and all-loving, why do people suffer? We would think that God would not allow it. The inspired author probed this mystery through a symbolic and imaginative story. In other words, the author probed this mystery through a myth.

The symbolic nature of the language is obvious. The garden contained a tree of life. As long as the man and woman could eat the fruit of this tree, they would not die. The garden also had a tree of the knowledge of good and evil. (You can read this story five hundred times and still not find an apple tree!) God told the man and the woman not to eat the fruit of this tree because if they did, on that day they would die. This plot detail gives us an insight into the real topic of the story. The man and woman disobeyed God and ate the fruit of the forbidden tree. Did they die? In one sense, they didn't. They were still physically alive. But in another sense they did. After they ate of the tree, all of their relationships were destroyed. This tells us that the story is not about physical life and death but about spiritual life and death.

Another obvious clue to the fact that we are dealing with a story that uses symbols to probe mystery is that God was presented anthropomorphically; that is, God was described as though he were a human being. Notice that God went to walk and talk with the man and woman every evening. God was not pictured as all-knowing. God figured out that the man was lonely and that it was not good for the man to be alone, so God created the animals and the birds to see if they might solve the problem. Only after none of them proved to be a partner did God create woman. When the man and woman ate from the forbidden tree, God knew nothing about it. God went for a walk and a talk just as always. The only reason God realized something was wrong was because the man hid. God asked, "Why are you hiding?" The man replied, "Because I am naked." God said, "Who told you that you are naked?" That was when God figured it out.

Through the use of a simple plot and obvious symbols, the author teaches a profound truth that people of every generation need to hear: Sin always results in suffering. Why? Because sin changes who we are, and therefore changes our ability to be in right relationship with God, others, and ourselves. To see how this teaching grows out of the story, we need only unpack the symbols.

The garden symbolizes a time and place of innocence before sin enters the picture. There was no suffering in this garden. The man was in right relationship with God, with whom he walked and talked each evening. He was in right relationship with his beloved partner. They were so close that they were like one person. He was in right relationship with himself. That was why he found no shame in his nakedness. He had no self-alienation. Finally, he was in right relationship with his environment. Everything he needed was available to him.

The tree of the knowledge of good and evil symbolizes the fact that there is a spiritual, moral order to the universe. Some things are all right to do; other things are not all right to do. Also, God has revealed this spiritual order to his people. God's motive in revealing the order is love. God does not want his beloved people to have a knowledge of evil and, in contrast to it, a knowledge of good once possessed but later lost. To avoid spiritual death, the man and the woman had to live within the revealed spiritual order.

The serpent symbolizes temptation. The serpent asked the woman if the man and woman could eat the fruit of any tree.

The woman was stricter than God. She said that they could eat from every tree but one: the tree of the knowledge of good and evil. They could not eat from that tree, nor touch it. The serpent got the woman to doubt God's goodness and suggested that God told the man and the woman not to eat of the fruit of that one tree because if they did, they would become like God. In other words, the serpent suggested that God wished to deprive the man and woman of something good rather than protect them from something harmful. As is always true with sin, for some reason, at the time, God's way didn't look so good. To the woman, and then the man, the fruit looked good, and so they ate it.

Eating the fruit symbolizes sinning. Eating is a wonderful symbol for sinning because, as is true with sin, what we eat becomes a part of who we are. We can be forgiven for sin. We can even end up a holier person after sinning than we were before. But we will never be the same person. What is the difference? The difference is the name of the forbidden tree: the knowledge of good and evil. When we know sin from personal experience, we perceive others and the world differently from how we perceived them before. Sin changes who we are and our ability to be in right relationship with God and others.

The broken relationships were immediate. The man hid from God, was ashamed of his nakedness, and blamed his partner. God did not stop loving the man and woman. God made clothes for both of them to cover their nakedness. In addition, God warned them about the inevitable suffering they had brought upon themselves. The man would work by the sweat of his brow, and the woman would long for her husband, but he would lord it over her. Even childbirth would be painful.

In other words, sin causes suffering. The author did not say that a world in which one person lords it over another is a world that represents God's order of creation. Rather, the author said that a world in which one person lords it over another is a world that is suffering the disorder caused by sin. God established a moral and spiritual order as part of creation. Whenever human beings act contrary to that order, the inevitable result is suffering.

The story of the man and woman in the garden teaches a universal truth. Its lesson, however, that sin inevitably causes suffering, is not a complete answer to the question, "If God is all loving and all powerful, why do human beings suffer?" The truth that the story teaches is an extremely important insight, but it is not the fullness of revelation in regard to suffering. As we discussed earlier, the author of the Book of Job, who lived some six hundred years after the author of this story, realized that not all suffering is due to sin. Even the author of Job, however, could not talk about the redemptive power of suffering. The fullness of revelation about the mystery of suffering comes only in the New Testament, after an innocent person named Jesus suffered, died, and rose from the dead.

A Look Back and a Look Forward

Is your understanding of the first three chapters of Genesis any different now than it was before reading this booklet? The reaction of students upon first being introduced to the richness of the contextualist method is often quite strong and equally divided between anger and amazement. Many people become angry because they feel betrayed that no one ever taught them this approach. They feel foolish having reached adulthood without growing beyond their childhood understanding of the stories. To comfort such people I try to point out that it is impossible, even harmful, to try to teach children what they, as adults, have just learned. The lack of sufficient education has been an institutional problem: We have not had good adult education about the Bible. Remember, though, that it is not too late to remedy the problem. That is what we are doing right now.

Along with anger and disappointment about time lost, many new adult students feel a deep gratitude for present insights and opportunities, and a real longing to learn more. The Bible is rich beyond our imagining. When we think that every part of the Bible deserves the attention that we just gave to the first three chapters of Genesis, we realize that we have a lifetime of exploring ahead of us. We need to read the text, let the text raise questions in our minds, and then use the contextualist method to seek out answers to those questions.

In the following chapters, we try to come to a deeper knowledge of basic biblical themes such as covenant and kingdom. In order to trace the development of thought in relation to these themes, we draw material first from one book and then another; we jump around in the library of the Bible. As we do that, we will have to hold ourselves accountable to the contextualist method that we have just learned. We cannot use a text for our own purposes unless the author of the text had the same purpose in mind. So we cannot use a text without answering the question, What was the original author of this text teaching the original audience? The authority of revelation can be found only in the context of that teaching. In order to determine what the author was teaching we consider contexts: the literary form, the beliefs of the time, and the process of revelation.

If we are faithful to our method, we will be able to help others—even terrorist bombers!—unlock the revelation in texts. We will be able to explain that the inspired human author of Exodus, who pictured God instructing the people to completely destroy their enemies, taught the people that *they* were in a relationship of covenant love with God and were beloved of God. The author, however, did not realize that God also loved Israel's enemies. The author lived before the Israelites grew to understand that God loved other nations too. This additional insight was learned just as the Babylonian exile (587–537 B.C.) was ending and is taught in the Book of Jonah (more about this later).

The statement that there is no greater love than to lay down one's life for one's friends is said in relation to Jesus' sacrifice for us. It refers to the fact that Jesus laid down his life in service and did not take back the gift of his life of service even after he realized that fidelity to his call might result in his being killed. The passage cannot be used to support the deliberate taking of one's own life.

We now move to the core concept that lies behind each of these two misinterpreted passages, and behind all of Scripture: the idea of covenant love. We discover that the whole story contained in the Bible, all two thousand years of it, reveals a growing realization of the ramifications of the facts that God is love, that God loves everyone, and that God wants us to learn to love one another.

FOR REFLECTION

1. Are you comfortable with the idea that any literary form, including myth, is an appropriate vehicle for revelation? Why or why not?

2. Do you believe that you are made in God's image? Do you believe that every person is made in God's image? What ramifications does this belief have in regard to your beliefs about the death penalty, euthanasia, and abortion? On what other issues does this belief affect your thinking?

3. Do you agree that sin always causes suffering? If so, why? What is it about sin that makes suffering inevitable?

CHAPTER 3

Covenant Love

"Comfort, O comfort my people, says your God" (Isaiah 40:1). These beautiful words from Isaiah express the constant, unwavering, and unending love that God has for his people. The two most important words are *my* and *your.* "Comfort my people says *your* God." Through the prophet, God assures the people of Judah, who have been in exile in Babylon, that he has not deserted them. God and the people still belong to each other. We cannot understand either the Old Testament or the New Testament unless we understand covenant love. In this chapter, we trace the development of the understanding of covenant love through the history of the Israelites. We see that all of the basic concepts that lie behind Scripture—concepts such as exodus, messiah, salvation, prophecy, conversion, and kingdom—are related to covenant love and are correctly understood only in the context of covenant love.

It is obvious that covenant love is the core concept of Scripture by the very fact that we refer to Scripture as the Old Testament and the New Testament. The words *covenant* and *testament* are synonyms. The Old Testament reveals the growing understanding of covenant that occurred over a period of nearly two thousand years. The events during those years, and the subsequent reflection upon the meaning of those events, provide us with the mental concepts and the vocabulary to begin understanding the meaning of the mysterious events that occurred in and through Jesus Christ. The Old Testament provides us with the cognitive stepping stones to understand the New Testament. What is "old" and "new" is not covenant love itself but our understanding of that love, a love that knows no bounds.

Covenant Love at the Time of Abraham and Beyond

The earliest historic person in the Old Testament is Abraham, our father in faith. We begin the story of Abraham in the twelfth chapter of Genesis. The preceding chapters set the stage, first by picturing God creating all that exists and seeing that it is all good, and then by describing the growing effects of sin. By the end of Genesis, chapter 11, it is clear that the human race needed to be saved and that the human race could not save itself. So, God called Abraham (Abram) and directed him to leave the land of his ancestors and go to a new land that God would show him. Abraham did what God told him to do.

The unique and overwhelming personal experience of God's presence in Abraham's life is described in terms of a covenant. We read about the terms of the covenant and the ritualization of the covenant in Genesis 15:1–21.

> After these things the word of the Lord came to Abram in a vision, "Do not be afraid, Abram, I am your shield; your reward shall be very great." But Abram said, "O Lord God, what will you give me, for I continue childless and the heir of my house is Eliezer of Damascus?" And Abram said, "You have given me no offspring, and so a slave born in my house is to be my heir." But the word of the Lord came to him, "This man shall not be your heir; no one but your very own issue shall be your heir." He brought him outside and said, "Look toward heaven and count the stars, if you are able to count them." Then he said to him, "So shall your descendants be." And he believed the Lord; and the Lord reckoned it to him as righteousness.

> Then he said to him, "I am the Lord who brought you from Ur of the Chaldeans, to give you this land to possess." But he said, "O Lord God, how am I to know that I shall possess it?" He said to him, "Bring me a heifer three years old, a female goat three years old, a ram three years old, a turtle-dove, and a young pigeon." He brought him all these and cut them in two, laying each half over

against the other; but he did not cut the birds in two. And when birds of prey came down on the carcasses, Abram drove them away.

As the sun was going down, a deep sleep fell upon Abram, and a deep and terrifying darkness descended upon him. Then the Lord said to Abram, "Know this for certain, that your offspring shall be aliens in a land that is not theirs, and shall be slaves there, and they shall be oppressed for four hundred years; but I will bring judgment on the nation that they serve, and afterward they shall come out with great possessions. As for yourself, you shall go to your ancestors in peace; you shall be buried in a good old age. And they shall come back here in the fourth generation; for the iniquity of the Amorites is not yet complete."

When the sun had gone down and it was dark, a smoking fire pot and a flaming torch passed between these pieces. On that day the Lord make a covenant with Abram, saying, "To your descendants I give this land, from the river of Egypt to the great river, the river Euphrates, the land of the Kenites, the Kenizzites, and Kadmonites, the Hittites, the Perizzites, the Rephaim, the Amorites, the Canaanites, the Girgashites, and the Jebusites."

To correctly understand this passage, we must remember everything we have already learned about how to correctly interpret Scripture. We must ask, What is the literary form of the passage I am reading? The literary form of this passage, and of many of the other passages we will read when we trace the idea of covenant, is legend. A legend is related to what we would call historical writing, but it is not identical to historical writing. A legend is defined as a symbolic and imaginative story with a historical base. The historical base of this legend is Abraham, who lived around 1850 B.C. and who, because of his personal relationship with God, had a profound effect not only on his contemporaries but on every generation since.

Legends differ from what we would consider historical writing in two ways. First, legends are based on oral tradition. This means that all we have learned about the effect of oral tradition on a text is applicable to this text. We can see that this text includes the point of view not only of the original audience but of later generations of storytellers as well, because the story includes knowledge of the history of the people through the Exodus experience. Because they are based on oral tradition, legends are often called folk history.

The second way in which legends differ from what we refer to as history is that legends are told not to re-create an event as it occurred but to teach the significance of the event to succeeding generations. Many legends are told to create heroes or to emphasize certain virtues. You are undoubtedly familiar with the legend about George Washington and a cherry tree that is told to teach the virtue of honesty. Because legends have a teaching function, the legend teller has permission to make the story as interesting as possible. Legends routinely include exaggeration, magical details, and accounts of folk customs appropriated for religious purposes. The legends about events in the Bible are told to teach the religious significance of the events. God is the hero. For this reason, they are often referred to as "religious history."

The religious significance of Abraham's personal experience of God's power and presence is understood and described in terms of "covenant": "The Lord made a covenant with Abram. . ." (Genesis 15:18). The idea of a covenant already existed in Abraham's culture. In Genesis we read of other covenants between human beings. For instance, Abraham made a covenant with Abimelech over a well (see 21:22–34). A covenant was the most solemn and binding of agreements. Because covenant agreements were so important, they were solemnized through ritual action, the specific mutual obligations of each person were spelled out, and the existence of the agreement was made concrete through external signs.

In the passage from Genesis 15 that we just read, we see most of the elements of covenant agreements. The agreement was solemnized through the ritual action of the cutting of the animals. In Abraham's time, in order to express the obligations inherent in covenant agreements, the two contracting parties would walk between the carcasses of cut animals as a way of expressing that they would rather be cut in half like these animals than break the agreement. The smoking fire pot and flaming torch that passed through the pieces of cut animals symbolized God's binding of himself to the agreement.

God's covenant with Abraham involved mutual responsibilities. God promised to protect Abraham and to give him land and descendants. Abraham was to have faith in God and obey.

A covenant agreement was an abstraction. The core of the agreement was the relationship itself. In order to concretize the reality of covenant love, some concrete ritual or sign was instituted. We read of such a sign in Abraham's covenant agreement with God in Genesis 17:9–13.

> God said to Abraham, "As for you, you shall keep my covenant, you and your offspring after you throughout their generations. This is my covenant, which you shall keep, between me and you and your offspring after you: Every male among you shall be circumcised. You shall circumcise the flesh of your foreskins, and it shall be a sign of the covenant between me and you. Throughout your generations every male among you shall be circumcised when he is eight days old, including the slave born in your house and the one bought with your money from any foreigner who is not of your offspring. Both the slave born in your house and the one bought with your money must be circumcised. So shall my covenant be in your flesh an everlasting covenant.

The whole Book of Genesis, indeed the whole Bible, is the story of the living out of covenant love. Abraham and his descendants understood themselves to be God's Chosen People. God promised to love and protect them. God promised to give them land. In return, the people had responsibilities to love and obey God. Through the years, an understanding of the ramifications of covenant love grew, but the basic concept remained firm, right up to our own day.

Covenant Love at the Time of Moses and Beyond

The Book of Exodus, the second book of the Bible, continues the story of covenant love. Six hundred years had passed since the time of Abraham. The Chosen People were in slavery in Egypt. The stories of their ancestors, however, and of their special relationship with a God who saves, were still very much alive. Covenant love formed an expectation that God would intervene in events to save his people. And God did. God called Moses. You are undoubtedly familiar with the story of the Exodus. The experience of slavery in Egypt; the plagues; the flight from that country; wandering in the desert; being fed with manna, quail, and water from the rock; receiving the Law; and finally arriving in the Promised Land—these were the core events that made up the most profound and formative time in salvation history before the coming of Jesus Christ. The whole experience was understood and interpreted in the context of covenant love. God was being faithful to his promises. God saw the people, his own people, in slavery, and took action to save them and to return them to the land that he had promised Abraham.

As a result of the Exodus experience, a growth in understanding of covenant love emerged, and new ways to concretize the reality of covenant love were established. The primary celebration that grew out of the Exodus experience was the Passover celebration. The Passover ritual is described in Exodus 12:1–14.

> *The Lord said to Moses and Aaron in the land of Egypt: This month shall mark for you the beginning*

of months; it shall be the first month of the year for you. Tell the whole congregation of Israel that on the tenth of this month they are to take a lamb for each family, a lamb for each household. If a household is too small for a whole lamb, it shall join its closest neighbor in obtaining one; the lamb shall be divided in proportion to the number of people who eat of it. Your lamb shall be without blemish, a year old male; you may take it from the sheep or from the goats. You shall keep it until the fourteenth day of this month; then the whole assembled congregation of Israel shall slaughter it at twilight. They shall take some of the blood and put it to the two doorposts and the lintel of the houses in which they eat it. They shall eat the lamb the same night; they shall eat it roasted over the fire with unleavened bread and bitter herbs. Do not eat any of it raw or boiled in water but roasted over the fire, with its head, legs, and inner organs. You shall let none of it remain until the morning; anything that remains until the morning you shall burn. This is how you shall eat it: your loins girded, your sandals on your feet, and your staff in your hand; and you shall eat it hurriedly. It is the passover of the Lord. For I will pass through the land of Egypt that night, and I will strike down every firstborn in the land of Egypt, both human beings and animals; on all the gods of Egypt I will execute judgments: I am the Lord. The blood shall be a sign for you on the houses where you live: When I see the blood, I will pass over you, and no plague shall destroy you when I strike the land of Egypt.

This day shall be a day of remembrance for you. You shall celebrate it as a festival to the Lord; throughout your generations you shall observe it as a perpetual ordinance.

According to the Gospels of Mark, Matthew, and Luke, Jesus celebrated the Passover meal the night before he died. The celebration, in accordance with tradition, involved a meal that included lamb and unleavened bread. The lamb was in memory of an earlier lamb, an actual four-legged animal that had been slaughtered and whose blood was placed on the lintels of the homes of the Israelites so that the angel of death would pass over those homes during the final plague. A lamb's blood had given life—extended life on the earth. The Gospel writers built on this image, a lamb whose blood gives life, when they proclaimed the Good News of salvation in Jesus Christ.

In addition to new celebrations of covenant love, the Exodus experience resulted in new understandings of the mutual responsibilities of covenant love. The people had received the Law; they now had a clearer understanding of just what obedience would involve. To concretize God's presence among his people, and the people's responsibility to act as God would have them act, the Law was transported with the people in its own tent. This traveling symbol of God's presence among them was called the ark of the Covenant.

Covenant Love at the Time of David and Beyond

A terrible thing happened to the Israelites some two hundred years after their arrival in the Promised Land. The Philistines, powerful enemies, stole the ark of the Covenant. What could this event possibly mean? After all, the ark was the concrete sign of God's covenant love.

Because of this event, many Israelites believed that they needed a tighter political organization rather than the loose confederacy of twelve tribes on which they had previously relied. Many believed that Israel, like other nations, should have a king. Saul was chosen as Israel's first king. The establishment of a king and a kingdom resulted in new understandings and new celebrations of covenant love.

The greatest king in Israel's history was their second king, David, who was understood to be an expression of covenant love. After all, God had promised to love and protect. The Philistines were threatening to destroy God's own people. If God were going to be faithful to his promise to protect, he would have to send someone to defeat the Philistines. And God did. He sent David.

David was anointed king by the prophet Samuel (see 1 Samuel 16:1–13). That means that David was a messiah. The word *messiah* and the word *Christ* both mean "anointed." David united the twelve tribes, defeated the Philistines, established his capital in Jerusalem, and brought the ark of the Covenant to Jerusalem. During the reign of David, the existence of a king and a kingdom began to be seen as the concrete signs of covenant love. We read of this understanding in 2 Samuel. David had been talking to the prophet Nathan about his desire to build God a house, a temple. After all, God deserved more than a tent. David discussed this idea with Nathan. At first, Nathan thought that David had a good idea. But that evening the Lord spoke to Nathan, and Nathan delivered God's message to the king (see 2 Samuel 7:8–14, 16).

When Jesus was alive and the Jews were under Roman rule, Jesus' contemporaries were expecting God to send a king of David's line, an anointed one, a messiah, to free them. This expectation had been present ever since the time of King David. Jesus would build on the image of an expected messiah, and of a kingdom, when he proclaimed that "the kingdom of God is at hand."

Covenant Love at the Time of the Prophet Hosea and Beyond

As we have discussed, kingship and prophecy are co-extensive. While some of the Israelites were adamant that Israel should have a king like other nations, others feared that if Israel had a king, the king might forget who is really king: God. Prophets existed to remind the king and the nation that God is king, and that everyone, including the king, must be faithful to covenant love.

One prophet, Hosea (745–722 B.C.), who called the Northern Kingdom to fidelity to covenant love, had an especially keen perception of one aspect of covenant love. Hosea had the horrible experience of being married to a woman who was repeatedly unfaithful to him. Hosea need not have put up with this situation; the Law would have allowed him to be rid of his unfaithful wife, to have her stoned to death. But Hosea could not bring himself to follow the Law. He could not stop hoping that his wife would change, and that instead of her being destroyed she would return to him in love and fidelity. As Hosea meditated on the meaning of his life, he came to the realization that he and his wife were a living metaphor of the relationship between God and Israel. God, too, is married to an unfaithful spouse. God, too, could choose to destroy. Because God loves, however, he does not want to destroy. Rather, God called his beloved to conversion and to receive her back in a relationship of mutual love and fidelity. Hosea pictured God wooing God's unfaithful spouse back to a loving relationship.

> Therefore, I will now allure her,
>> and bring her into the wilderness,
>> and speak tenderly to her.
> From there I will give her her vineyards,
>> and make the Valley of Achor a door of hope.
> There she shall respond as in the days of her youth,
>> as at the time when she came out of the land of Egypt.

> On that day, says the Lord, you will call me, "My husband," and no longer will you call me, "My Baal." For I will remove the names of the Baals from her mouth, and they shall be mentioned by name no more. I will make for you a covenant on that day with the wild animals, the birds of the air, and the

creeping things of the ground; and I will abolish the
bow, the sword, and war from the land; and I will
make you lie down in safety. And I will take you for
my wife forever; I will take you for my wife in right-
eousness and in justice, in steadfast love, and in
mercy. I will take you for my wife in faithfulness;
and you shall know the Lord.

(Hosea 2:14–20)

Hosea understood that God simply cannot stop loving. Because God cannot stop loving, Hosea, who spoke in God's name, would have two main messages. One message is "Repent!" Prophets always called people to repentance because they understood that sin was contrary to covenant love and could result only in suffering. The prophets, however, always had a second message: "Have hope!" It was always realistic to have hope, no matter what the circumstances might be, because God had promised to love, and he would keep that promise. God had not promised to love only if his people remained faithful. God had promised to love under every circumstance. Because it was God's nature to love and to save, he could not do otherwise.

From the time of the establishment of the kingdom through the Babylonian exile, the prophets continued to call God's people to fidelity to covenant love. Often the message was a call to repentance. The prophets constantly reminded both the king and the nation of their obligations to obey the Law, to love God, and to love one another. Right behavior was the social expression of covenant love.

During times of suffering, however, the prophets constantly reminded the people to have hope. God had promised to save, and he would save. God would send one like David, a promised messiah, to save God's people from their political enemies. It was the prophetic message of hope that we read as we began this chapter: "Comfort, O comfort my people, says your God."

Covenant Love at the Time
of the Babylonian Exile and Beyond

The experience of the Babylonian exile challenged every belief that the people had in regard to covenant love. Since the time of King David, the concrete signs of covenant love had been seen as the king, the kingdom, and the Temple. Even after the Northern Kingdom had been destroyed by the Assyrians, the people of the Southern Kingdom continued to believe that they were invulnerable to their enemies because God had promised that their king and their nation would be secure forever. The prophet Jeremiah realized that this understanding was a mistake. The core of covenant love was a right relationship with God. The externals of king, kingdom, and Temple were signs of that right relationship. If, in fact, a right relationship did not exist, these signs lost their meaning and might well be destroyed. Jeremiah declared as false prophets those who comforted the people by saying that no harm would come to them.

> *Thus says the Lord of hosts: Do not listen to the words of the prophets who prophesy to you; they are deluding you. They speak visions of their own minds, not from the mouth of the Lord. They keep saying to those who despise the word of the Lord, "It shall be well with you"; and to all who stubbornly follow their own stubborn hearts, they say, "No calamity shall come upon you."*
>
> (Jeremiah 23:16–17).

Jeremiah did not tell the people that God would desert them. Rather, he said that God wanted to be in right relationship with them. The hardening of their hearts, accompanied by external signs of covenant love, could not continue. God would call the people back to himself through the experience of the Exile (see Jeremiah 31:31–34).

Events proved Jeremiah correct in his belief that the king, kingdom, and Temple were all vulnerable to destruction. Indeed, all were destroyed by the conquering Babylonians. The king's sons were killed, and he himself, along with the upper-class population of Jerusalem, were led into exile. The Temple was destroyed. Not only were the people and the land devastated but so was the people's idea of covenant love. Did this horrible course of events mean that God had broken his promise? Did it mean that they were no longer God's people? The traumatizing events of the Babylonian exile forced the people to re-examine their idea of covenant love. In that re-examination, new depths of understanding were reached and the ground was laid for the revelation of God's covenant love that would occur through Jesus Christ.

Before we move on to the post-Babylonian exile understanding of covenant love, we should pause for a moment to notice the literary form of the passages that we have quoted from the prophets Nathan, Hosea, and Jeremiah. Notice that the prophets attributed their words directly to God, beginning with the words, "Yahweh says this . . . ." To say, "Yahweh says this," and then to attribute words directly to God, was not to claim exact quotations but to use the literary form "oracle."

The prophets employed a number of different literary forms as they passed on their keen spiritual insights to their contemporaries, but the most commonly used form was the oracle. This form presupposed the true function of a prophet. The word prophet means "one who speaks for another." In the context of the Bible, the "other" was God. So a prophet was one who spoke for God. The gift of a prophet was not, as many people assume, the gift to prognosticate inevitable future events. Rather, the gift of the prophet was to correctly understand covenant love and to correctly judge the ramifications of present behavior in the light of covenant love. The prophet spoke for God as the prophet called the people to conversion and reminded them to remain hopeful because God loved and saved. Because the prophet spoke for God, the prophet attributed his words to God, using the literary form that we call oracle.

Post-Babylonian Exile Insights Regarding Covenant Love

The events of the Babylonian exile caused people to reflect on two mysteries of God's love: God loves everyone, and suffering is not always punishment.

GOD LOVES EVERYONE

The Babylonian exile ended in a most unexpected way. Cyrus, who was a Persian, conquered the Babylonians and allowed the exiles to return home. It was not that the exiles did not expect that God would send a messiah, an anointed one, to save them. This expectation was part and parcel of covenant love. The exiles expected that God would send someone like Moses or David to save them—one of their own. That a foreigner, not even a member of God's Chosen People, would be called by God as an instrument of his saving power was beyond belief! But it happened. What could this mean?

The prophet known as second Isaiah *(see Isaiah 40–55)*, who lived during the Babylonian exile, reflected on this experience. He believed that God used world events to bring about his will for the Chosen People:

> Thus says the Lord to his anointed, to Cyrus. . . .
> For the sake of my servant Jacob,
>   and Israel my chosen,
> I call you by your name,
>   I surname you, though you do not know me.
> I am the Lord, and there is no other;
>   besides me there is no god.
>   I arm you, though you do not know me,
> so that they may know, from the rising of the sun
>   and from the west, that there is no one besides me;
>   I am the Lord, and there is no other.
>
> (Isaiah 45:1, 4–6)

Events led the people to ask, "If God used a person from another nation to accomplish his will, does that mean that God loves people of other nations?"

Another inspired author, who lived after the Babylonian exile, reflected upon these same events and came to an amazing and alarming conclusion. If God used other nations as instruments of his saving power, then God must love other nations. After all, there was no other God. God made these other nations. God called these other nations to do his will. God must love these other nations. This was a great, but unwelcome, insight. Who wants to believe that God loves our enemies as much as he loves us?

In order to teach his contemporaries that God loved other nations, the author wrote the Book of Jonah. This very short book, which appears with the prophetic books in the edited arrangement of the Old Testament, is a work of didactic fiction. That is, the author composed a humorous and ironic story in order to teach a serious lesson to a resistant audience. The setting of the book is several hundred years earlier than the time of the author, during the time when Assyria, not Babylon or Persia, was the political enemy. Nineveh, the city to which Jonah was sent, was the capital of Assyria, the nation that had conquered the Northern Kingdom.

The author began his story by picturing God sending his prophet, Jonah, to preach to the Ninevites. Jonah fled. After all, who would want to preach to the enemy? Who wants the enemy to be saved? No one, however, can flee from God. God arranged events so that a fish swallowed Jonah. While inside the fish, Jonah had a conversion and prayed to God in a beautiful psalm of thanksgiving. God heard Jonah, spoke to the fish, and had the fish vomit Jonah onto dry land.

The Lord called Jonah a second time to preach to the Ninevites. This time Jonah obeyed. He entered the city and proclaimed a single sentence: "Forty days more and Nineveh will be overthrown" (Jonah 3:4). Everyone heard and converted. All the people, great and small, converted. The king converted. Even the animals wore sackcloth and ashes.

Obviously, we are not reading history. Had the fictional setting of Jonah praying from the fish's belly not informed us of the literary form, the claim that all of Nineveh turned to the Lord certainly does.

INSIGHT INTO COVENANT LOVE

One would think that if God used a person as an instrument of salvation for a great nation, that person would be pleased. Jonah was not. Jonah was angry. Why? Because Jonah wanted the Ninevites destroyed. After all, they were the enemy. Jonah explained to God why he was so angry.

> *"O Lord! Is not this what I said while I was still in my own country? That is why I fled to Tarshish at the beginning; for I knew that you are a gracious God and merciful, slow to anger, and abounding in steadfast love, and ready to relent from punishing."*
>
> (Jonah 4:2)

The tone of these words is not praise but accusation. Jonah was angry because God was more loving than Jonah wanted God to be.

God then arranged events so as to teach Jonah why God loved the Ninevites. First God arranged for a little shade tree to grow up to protect Jonah from the heat. Then God arranged for a worm to eat the shade tree. Next, God arranged for a hot wind to cause Jonah even more discomfort. Jonah wanted to die. Obviously, Jonah was a parody of a prophet, not a historical prophet. The prophets endured terrible suffering for the Lord and persevered in order to be faithful to God's word. Jonah wanted to die because he was hot and angry. Then the Lord pointed out that although Jonah did not make the tree, he cared greatly that it had been destroyed. Isn't it possible that God would feel bad if the Ninevites were destroyed? After all, God did make the Ninevites.

The author of Jonah used a humorous work of fiction to try to get around the defenses of an audience for whom his message would be unwelcome. God loves other nations, even our enemies. This insight was a great step forward in understanding covenant love.

Suffering Is Not Always Punishment

The time of exile had been a time of terrible suffering. The prophet known as second Isaiah, in the very oracle with which we began this chapter, named the problem.

> Comfort, O comfort my people,
>> says your God.
> Speak tenderly to Jerusalem,
>> and cry to her
> that she has served her term,
>> that her penalty is paid,
> that she has received from the Lord's hand
>> double for all her sins.

(Isaiah 40:1–2)

Had the Lord let the people suffer so much to punish them for sin? Surely sin did cause suffering. But did it cause this much suffering? If all suffering was punishment for sin, the Lord seemed to have gone overboard on this one. The punishment didn't fit the crime.

In the face of this mystery, second Isaiah suggested a reason for suffering other than punishment for sin. Isaiah suggested that perhaps the Lord was using the suffering of the Chosen People for the good of other nations. Perhaps other nations would come to know God through the suffering and restoration of the Chosen People. Isaiah offered this hope and comfort to the people in one of his servant songs, songs in which the nation Israel was seen as the servant of God's will. Isaiah pictured the kings of other nations observing the servant nation with these words:

> But he [i.e. the nation Judah] was wounded for
>> our transgressions,
>> crushed for our iniquities;
> upon him was the punishment that made us
>> whole,
>> and by his bruises we are healed.

(Isaiah 53:5)

Perhaps suffering was not just punishment for sin. Perhaps suffering could have a saving effect.

THE BOOK OF JOB

As we discussed in chapter 2, the author of the Book of Job disagreed with his contemporaries on the meaning of suffering. They held that all suffering was due to sin. The contemporaries believed they were defending God's reputation by holding on to this belief. After all, if God was both all-loving and all-powerful, suffering had to be deserved. If it wasn't deserved, then God was either not all-loving or not all-powerful.

The author of the Book of Job chose the literary form of a debate to explore the question. To frame his debate, he used an old legend in which a character named Job, known for his goodness, is allowed to undergo suffering as a test. The legend frame established two facts: Job was innocent, and Job was suffering.

The debate took place because Job's friends, who witnessed his suffering, discussed with Job the reasons for his suffering. They each arrived at the same conclusion: Job must have sinned, otherwise he would not be suffering. The audience, of course, knew from the frame that the friends were wrong. God had said that Job was a good person. There had to be some reason for Job's sufferings other than punishment. Finally, God appeared to Job and his friends. The very fact that God appeared illustrated that God still loved Job. In fact, God affirmed Job's goodness but was angry with Job's friends.

> . . . the Lord said to Eliphaz the Temanite, "My wrath is kindled against you and against your two friends; for you have not spoken of me what is right, as my servant Job has."
>
> (Job 42:7)

A DEEP MYSTERY

The author of Job pointed out that insisting that all suffering is punishment for sin in order to defend God's reputation would have the opposite effect. All suffering could not be punishment for sin if God was all loving, because suffering often exceeded what love would allow. There was a deep mystery here that could not be solved. But to insist that all suffering was punishment for sin was to picture God as less loving than God actually was.

We see, then, that the experience of suffering caused by the Babylonian exile, and reflection on that suffering by inspired biblical authors, resulted in a deeper understanding of covenant love. God's love was greater and more mysterious than had previously been understood. God loved every single person—all nations—and God loved too much to actually inflict as punishment all of the suffering that people endure. Suffering must have some deeper, perhaps even some redemptive, purpose.

The Old Covenant and the New

Were it not for the covenant relationship of the Old Testament— for all the experiences, insights, explanations, and images that grew out of those explanations—the human race would never have been able to understand the Good News that was revealed through Jesus Christ. Both our understanding of covenant love and our celebrations of covenant love grew out of the Old Testament experience.

In the Gospels of Matthew, Mark, and Luke, Jesus ate the Passover meal with his disciples the night before he died (see Luke 22:14–20). We Christians, in remembrance of Jesus Christ, receive Christ's Body and Blood at our eucharistic celebration, the Mass. Just as Passover was Jesus' covenant-renewal ceremony, so the Mass is our covenant-renewal ceremony. We have appropriated and reinterpreted all the understandings and images of our ancestors in faith to celebrate and commit ourselves to covenant love. As we gather, we think of ourselves as God's holy temple, as the place where God dwells. We listen to the Word of God to remind ourselves of our obligations to act lovingly. We express our belief that a king of David's line has already saved us and will come again to judge the living and the dead. We pray that God's kingdom will come—not a geopolitical kingdom but an eternal kingdom. We behold the Lamb of God, and celebrate our belief that the Lamb's blood has given us life—eternal life. The concrete realities of the Old Testament experience have become the metaphors, the cognitive stepping-stones, to name and celebrate spiritual realities that are beyond our perception or our complete understanding.

The ramifications of covenant love, God's love for us and our love for God, are still beyond our ability to completely understand. We do understand, nevertheless, that covenant love is the core reality of our religious experience, just as it was for those who preceded us in faith.

FOR REFLECTION

1. Do you think of yourself as being in a relationship of covenant love with God? If so, what have you promised God? What do you think God has promised you? How do you ritualize and celebrate your love?

2. Do you understand yourself to be in a relationship of covenant love with any person? with your spouse? with your children? with your parents? with the Church? What are the ramifications of seeing these relationships in the context of covenant love?

3. Do you think there is a purpose for suffering beyond punishment? What is it?

CHAPTER 4

The Kingdom of God

The Gospel according to Mark, the earliest of the four canonical Gospels (65 A.D.), pictures Jesus beginning his public ministry with the words, "The time is fulfilled, and the kingdom of God has come near; repent, and believe the good news" (1:15). The Gospel according to Matthew (80 A.D.), which used Mark as a source, pictures Jesus' public ministry beginning with similar words: "Repent, for the kingdom of heaven has come near" (4:17). The Gospel according to Luke (85 A.D.), which also used Mark as a source, pictures Jesus beginning his public ministry with the words,

> "The Spirit of the Lord is upon me,
>   because he has anointed me
>   to bring good news to the poor.
> He has sent me to proclaim release to the captives
>   and recovery of sight to the blind,
>   to let the oppressed go free,
>   to proclaim the year of the Lord's favor."

(4:18–19)

As you can see, these three Gospels, referred to as the synoptic Gospels because of their similarity to one another, picture Jesus as preaching primarily not about himself but about the kingdom of God. As you know from our first chapter, in which we described the five-step process that resulted in the Gospels as we now have them, Jesus, as a historical person, had a different point of view during his public ministry than did the Gospel editors. Jesus preached from a pre-Resurrection point of view; the Gospel editors wrote from a post-Resurrection point of view. Jesus focused on the kingdom of God; the Gospel editors focused on the person of Jesus Christ.

Because the concept of the kingdom of God was central to Jesus' preaching, we devote this chapter to exploring just what Jesus tried to teach us about the kingdom of God. In our next chapter we take the post-Resurrection point of view of the Gospel editors and explore the question, Who is Jesus Christ? In the course of both explorations, we will have the opportunity to see once more how essential our contextualist approach to the Bible is in understanding the revelation that Scripture contains.

Understanding "Kingdom"

When we participate in our covenant-renewal ceremony, the Mass, we say together what we have come to call the Lord's Prayer or the Our Father. This prayer is called the Lord's Prayer because it is based on a prayer that Jesus taught his disciples in Matthew's and Luke's Gospels. In Matthew's Gospel Jesus began the prayer with the words.

> *"Our Father in heaven,*
> *hallowed be your name.*
> *Your kingdom come.*
> *Your will be done,*
> *on earth as it is in heaven."*

(6:9–10)

Jesus taught his disciples to pray for the coming of the kingdom, but what did Jesus' disciples understand by the word *kingdom*? We already know that the idea of a kingdom was a central component in the Israelites' understanding of covenant love. The kingdom, the king, and the Temple were understood to be the external signs of God's covenant promises to love and protect the Chosen People. When Jesus' contemporaries thought of a kingdom, they thought of a geopolitical reality, of a nation located on the eastern shore of the Mediterranean Sea. Their idea of a messiah, an anointed one whom God would send to defeat their political enemies, was closely connected to their idea of kingdom.

It is evident that some of Jesus' listeners understood the word *kingdom* in the geopolitical sense. The mother of the sons of Zebedee, for example, certainly understood Jesus to be speaking of a geopolitical reality; otherwise she would never have said, "Declare that these two sons of mine will sit, one at your right hand and one at your left, in your kingdom" (Matthew 20:21). Many in the crowd who welcomed Jesus into the city of

Jerusalem before his Passion were also thinking of a geopolitical reality; otherwise they never would have said, "Hosanna! Blessed is the one who comes in the name of the Lord! Blessed is the coming kingdom of our ancestor David! Hosanna in the highest heaven" (Mark 11:9–10).

This misunderstanding must have been terribly frustrating for Jesus, because the reality to which he was referring was not a geopolitical reality at all but a spiritual and eternal reality. Jesus used the word *kingdom* as a metaphor to describe something that was beyond the perception of his listeners. He described a kingdom in which God's will would reign: "Thy kingdom come; thy will be done." Jesus had come to announce and to initiate the imminent in-breaking of the kingdom of God. "Repent, for the kingdom of heaven has come near" (Matthew 4:17).

You may have noticed that where Mark says, "the kingdom of God," Matthew, in parallel passages, says, "the kingdom of heaven" (see Mark 1:15; Matthew 4:17). Matthew did not intend to introduce a new concept with this change of wording; he wanted to be responsive to the sensitivities of his audience. Matthew's audience was primarily made up of Jews who refrained from naming God out of a deep awe of God's greatness. Matthew, therefore, pictured Jesus saying, "kingdom of heaven," rather than "kingdom of God." Sometimes, however, the effect of this change was to cause further misunderstanding about Jesus' intent when he spoke of the kingdom of God. For many, "heaven" was understood to be a place where good persons went after they left the earth. For such persons, then, the words "kingdom of heaven" or "kingdom of God" would refer to a spiritual reality but one that cannot be entered until after death. This, too, seemed to be quite a different idea from the one that Jesus proclaimed. Jesus taught his disciples to pray that the kingdom will be present "on earth as it is in heaven" (Matthew 6:10). What, then, did Jesus mean by the word "kingdom"?

Because the kingdom was such a mysterious reality, Jesus taught about the kingdom through parables. Many of Jesus' parables began, "the kingdom of God is like . . . ." So, in order to understand what Jesus was trying to teach us about the kingdom through his parables, we must say a few words about the literary form of the parable.

What Is a Parable?

A parable, at its root, is a comparison. Like any good teacher, Jesus explained what was beyond human comprehension by comparing it to something with which we are familiar. The comparison in a true parable, however, is between someone or something in the story and the audience listening to the story. The function of a parable is not only to teach the audience but also to call the audience to conversion. All of this is best explained by example.

THE PARABLE OF THE LABORERS IN THE VINEYARD

One parable through which Jesus taught his disciples about the kingdom of God was the parable of the laborers in the vineyard. Jesus began, "For the kingdom of heaven is like a landowner who went out early in the morning to hire laborers for his vineyard . . ." (see Matthew 20:1–15). Jesus continues by telling a story in which workers were hired to work for the entire day, from noon on, and for an hour at the end of the day. The all-day workers agreed to a daily wage. At the end of the day, the vineyard owner paid the workers in the opposite order from the order in which they were hired. When the all-day workers saw that the one-hour workers were paid what they had been promised for a whole day's work, they expected to be paid more than their original agreement but they were not. They became angry because those who worked less were paid the same amount. What was Jesus teaching about the kingdom by telling this story?

In order to interpret the story, we must remember that the lesson in a parable is drawn by comparing someone or something in the story to the audience to whom the story is told. We need to go back to the text and find out to whom Jesus told the story and why. Once the parable is put into the context in which it appears in Matthew's Gospel, we see that it is part of a long eschatological (i.e., about the end times) sermon that Jesus gave his disciples. Peter had said to Jesus, "Look, we have left everything and followed you. What then will we have?" (Matthew 19:27). Jesus told the parable of the vineyard workers as part of his response to Peter's question.

Behind Peter's question Jesus heard a presumption about the kingdom of God that is in error. Through the parable, Jesus challenged that presumption and called Peter to conversion. Peter's false presumption was that the kingdom was something that he and the other disciples were earning rather than something they were receiving as a gift. To challenge this presumption, Jesus told a story that violated the sense that a person gets what a person earns. Peter and the disciples were like the vineyard workers who were invited into the vineyard: No one earned the invitation. In addition, no one received less than he earned. Everyone was paid the agreed upon daily wage. The problem was that some people received more than they earned.

This is the way it is with the kingdom. No one earns the kingdom. Everyone receives it as a gift. If there are complaints to be made, it can only be because the owner of the vineyard is too generous!

THE PARABLE OF THE WEDDING BANQUET

Every insight that we learn about the kingdom through Jesus' parables raises another question. The parable of the vineyard workers teaches us that the kingdom is not earned. Does this mean that a person's response to Jesus' good news about the kingdom is irrelevant? Obviously not, since the good news is preceded by the word "Repent!" A person's response is all-important. Jesus taught this truth through this parable.

Once again the parable began, "The kingdom of heaven may be compared to a king who gave a wedding banquet for his son . . ." (see Matthew 22:1–13). Jesus went on to tell a story in which those who were invited to the wedding banquet refused to come. In response to their refusal, the king told his slaves to go out to the streets and gather all the people they found, both good and bad, in order to fill the hall with guests.

> *"But when the king came in to see the guests, he noticed a man there who was not wearing a wedding robe, and he said to him, 'Friend, how did you get in here without a wedding robe?' And he was speechless. Then the king said to the attendants, 'Bind him hand and foot, and throw him into the outer darkness, where there will be weeping and gnashing of teeth.'"*

> (Matthew 22:11–13)

What was Jesus teaching about the kingdom of God through this parable? Once again we must interpret the parable as a parable in order to find the revelation that it contains. To whom was Jesus telling this story and why? Jesus told this story to the chief priests and the Pharisees. Jesus had just told them another parable, the parable of the wicked tenants, which they recognized as being aimed at them. The chief priests and Pharisees wanted to arrest Jesus, but they were afraid of the crowd. The chief priests and Pharisees were compared to the guest who appeared to be accepting the invitation to the kingdom, but who, in fact, was not. His lack of proper response amounted to his refusing the invitation.

Notice that in the story everyone was invited to the banquet. Some refused outright; others appeared to respond to the invitation, but in reality they did not. The guest who was thrown out symbolized such a person, a person just like the chief priests and Pharisees. He was thrown out of the banquet not only because of his lack of proper dress but also because of his unwillingness to enter into conversation with the king, who addressed him as "friend." Jesus was teaching the chief priests and Pharisees that while they might consider themselves to be among the chosen, and believe that they are responding to the invitation to the kingdom of God, in reality they are not. Their failure to respond to what Jesus was teaching them would result in their being excluded from the kingdom.

THE PARABLE OF THE FIG TREE

If a person refuses the invitation to the kingdom, is that person excluded forever? Are there any second chances? This seems to be the question that Jesus addressed when he told the parable of the fig tree.

> "A man had a fig tree planted in his vineyard; and he came looking for fruit on it and found none. So he said to the gardener, 'See here! For three years I have come looking for fruit on this fig tree, and still I find none. Cut it down! Why should it be wasting the soil?' He replied, 'Sir, let it alone for one more year, until I dig around it and put manure on it. If it bears fruit next year, well and good; but if not, you can cut it down.'"
>
> (Luke 13:6–9)

Jesus told this story to a crowd he accused of being unable to read the signs of the times (see Luke 12:56). Some in the crowd had told Jesus how others had met with sudden death (see Luke 13:1). Jesus urged his listeners to repent while there was still time. Although their opportunity to repent was not over, repentance was nevertheless an urgent matter, since no one knew how long one could postpone repentance without risking destruction.

When Will the Kingdom Come?

The fact that there was an urgent need to respond to the invitation to the kingdom caused Jesus' listeners to ask, "When will the kingdom come?"

> Once Jesus was asked by the Pharisees when the kingdom of God was coming, and he answered, "The kingdom of God is not coming with things that can be observed; nor will they say, 'Look, here it is!'

or 'There it is!' For, in fact, the kingdom of God is among you."

(Luke 17:20–21)

THE PARABLES OF THE MUSTARD SEED AND THE YEAST

The idea that the kingdom of God was not only a future, external reality but also a present, internal reality was important to Jesus. Jesus never denied that the reality of the kingdom was not wholly present. He did not discourage people from thinking in terms of a future, culminating, event in which they would see "the Son of Man coming on the clouds of heaven with power and great glory" (Matthew 24:30). Jesus, however, also emphasized the present reality of the kingdom and the fact that its presence and growth could go undetected. This seemed to be Jesus' emphasis when he told the parables of the mustard seed and the yeast.

> "The kingdom of heaven is like a mustard seed that someone took and sowed in his field; it is the smallest of all the seeds, but when it has grown it is the greatest of shrubs and becomes a tree, so that the birds of the air come and make nests in its branches." He told them another parable: "The kingdom of heaven is like yeast that a woman took and mixed in with three measures of flour until all of it was leavened."

(Matthew 13:31–33)

If one always thinks in terms of the future and of extraordinary events, one might miss the coming of the kingdom. The kingdom, in some sense, is already present.

You may have noticed that in interpreting the parable of the mustard seed and the parable of the yeast, we did not use the method we explained earlier, nor did we claim that the function of these two parables was to call the person to whom they were addressed to personal conversion. Not everything that is called a parable in Scripture is a true parable in the way in which we previously defined it.

The explanation for the lack of preciseness in the way the word *parable* is used in the Gospels lies in the mixture of the Hebrew and Greek cultures that took place in the last three hundred years before Jesus' birth. Parables were part of Jesus' Israelite heritage. We see others who preceded Jesus use the same form. The prophet Nathan, for example, told a parable to confront David with his sin of adultery (see 2 Samuel 12:1–4). As you already know, several hundred years before Jesus' birth, the Old Testament was translated into Greek (the Septuagint). The Greek word for parable was used to translate the Hebrew word *mashal*. A *mashal* could be a short, pithy saying or a long, developed allegory. So the word *parable* appears in our Bibles to name not only true parables, in terms of literary form, but also extended similes and even allegories.

Although the distinction among these literary forms is blurred in the biblical text, it is still important for us to recognize the difference. To interpret a parable as though it were an allegory can lead to serious error. In order to point out the danger, we must first define *allegory*. An allegory is a story that has two levels of meaning: the literal, or surface, level and the intentional level. Everything on the surface level stands for something on the intentional level. So the correct interpretation of an allegory rests on understanding a series of comparisons.

Allegories were common in Greek culture. As Jesus' parables passed through oral tradition, the settings of his stories were not always passed on. Remember that the loss of original social context is a characteristic of literature that passes through oral tradition. The early Church sometimes used Jesus' parables not as parables but as allegories. That is why, in a few instances, we find an allegorical sermon based on a parable included in the Gospels.

THE PARABLE OF THE SOWER

The parable of the sower is a good example (see Mark 4:1–9, 14–20). When Jesus told the parable of the sower to a crowd, there was urgency in his message: "Let anyone with ears to hear listen!" The crowd was compared to the soil. Jesus urged the crowd to convert and be "good soil." Later, Jesus was pictured giving an allegorical interpretation of the parable. The seed stood for the Word. The seed sown on rocky ground stood for people who . . . . The seed sown among thorns stood for people who . . . . Each plot element on the literal level of the story stood for something on the intentional level. The story was not about farming; it was about various people's receptivity to the Word of God.

THE PARABLE OF THE PRODIGAL SON

Because the Gospels themselves allegorize parables, it is not always wrong for us to do the same. Sometimes the lesson drawn from allegorizing a parable is compatible with what the Gospel teaches. An example is the parable of the prodigal son (see Luke 15:11–32). Jesus told this parable to the Pharisees and scribes who were complaining that Jesus spent too much time with sinners (see Luke 15:1). Jesus compared the Pharisees and scribes to the older brother whose self-righteous and judgmental attitudes left him incapable of loving his own brother. If we allegorize the parable, each character on the literal level stands for someone on the intentional level. The father in the story stands for God; the two brothers stand for two sinners. God loves and forgives sinners.

THE PARABLE OF THE UNJUST JUDGE

Sometimes, however, the message drawn from allegorizing parables is not compatible with the Gospel, and this error is the source of many mistaken interpretations. When Jesus taught his disciples to persevere in prayer, he told them a story about a woman and an unjust judge (see Luke 18:1–5). The woman was comparable to the disciples in that she needed something that another had the power to grant. If we allegorize the parable, however, the unjust judge would stand for God. Obviously, this is wrong.

THE PARABLE OF THE TALENTS

People often allegorize parables without realizing that's what they're doing. In the process, they compare God to the master in Jesus' parables—and the masters often were not admirable characters. Take the parable of the talents, for example (see Luke 19:12–27). This parable was meant to teach the disciples that they should not, out of fear, fail to use whatever talents they had been given as they waited for the coming of the kingdom. The master in the story, however, was harsh. As his servant said, "I was afraid of you, because you are a harsh man; you take what you did not deposit, and reap what you did not sow" (Luke19:21). Obviously, this is not the picture of God that the Gospels teach, but it is nevertheless the picture of God that many people have. The idea of God as being less than loving rests on a misinterpretation.

How Will We Recognize the Coming of the Kingdom?

As we have already noted, Jesus taught his disciples to pray, "Thy kingdom come. Thy will be done, on earth as it is in heaven." We also have noted how Luke pictured Jesus beginning his public ministry (see Luke 4:18–19).

We can tell that it was a deliberate choice of Luke's to make these the first words of Jesus' public ministry, because they are not the same words with which Jesus began his public ministry in Mark's Gospel, Luke's source. Mark pictured Jesus saying, "The time is fulfilled, and the kingdom of God has come near; repent, and believe in the good news" (1:15).

Luke placed these words on Jesus' lips because Luke was emphasizing Jesus' self-understanding: Jesus was not only announcing that the kingdom of God was at hand but he was making the kingdom's presence visible by freeing captives, returning sight to the blind, and letting the oppressed go free.

Jesus was announcing the presence of God's kingdom not only through his parables but through his mighty signs—his miracles. In Jesus' ministry, as distinct from the later Gospel narratives about Jesus, the mighty signs were one more way to preach about the presence of God's kingdom. Only in the light of the Resurrection are the miracle stories used to address the question, Who is this Jesus that he exhibits such power?

THE PARABLE OF THE JUDGMENT OF THE NATIONS

Just as Jesus wanted to make the presence of the kingdom visible to his contemporaries by being an instrument of God's love to the disadvantaged, so did he teach his followers to do the same. This was the lesson behind the parable of the judgment of the nations (see Matthew 25:31–46).

The parable of the judgment of the nations was one in a series in which Jesus taught about the coming of the kingdom of God. The question of *when* had come up again (see Matthew 24:3). Jesus talked about the signs that would precede the end, but he did not seem to think that the question of time was the most important issue. He told the disciples the parable of the ten bridesmaids (see Matthew 25:1–13) to teach them that they should always be ready. Next, he told the parable of the talents (see Matthew 25:14–30). As you know, this parable taught the disciples that they should not, out of fear, fail to use the "talents" that the master had given them while they waited for the coming of the kingdom.

Finally, Jesus told the parable of the judgment of the nations. The disciples are compared to those on the king's right and left who were being held accountable for their actions. They were being taught that they should spend their time feeding the hungry, clothing the naked, caring for the sick, welcoming the stranger, visiting those in prison—doing all they could to free the oppressed from whatever was oppressing them. In other words, as the disciples joined Jesus in his ministry, they were to proclaim the coming of the kingdom not only in words but in action. They were to be instruments of God's love in the lives of all those they met.

Paradoxes About the Kingdom

As Jesus taught his disciples about the kingdom, he called them into a world of paradox. Is the coming of the kingdom an event in the future or a present reality? It is both. Will the signs of the coming of the kingdom be dramatic and external or subtle and internal? They will be both. Is the kingdom a gift, or do we need to do something to receive it? Both. In preparation for the kingdom, should we think in terms of a final judgment or be ready now? Both. Is the invitation to the kingdom urgent or constant? Both. Is the kingdom a place we enter at death or is it a relationship that we enter when we begin to let God's will reign in our lives? Both. A full and complete understanding of kingdom is beyond our comprehension. That is why Jesus used parables to teach us about the kingdom. Each parable gives us a glimpse of one more truth about the mysterious reality that is the kingdom of God.

The Return of the Son of Man

Jesus' disciples expected him to return in glory on the clouds of heaven to judge the living and the dead during their lifetime. In Matthew's Gospel, when speaking of the end times, Jesus said:

> *"Immediately after the suffering of those days*
> *the sun will be darkened,*
>> *and the moon will not give its light;*
>> *the stars will fall from heaven,*
>>> *and the powers of heaven will be shaken.*
>
> *Then the sign of the Son of Man will appear in heaven, and then all the tribes of the earth will mourn and they will see 'the Son of Man coming on the clouds of heaven' with power and great glory. And he will send out his angels with a loud trumpet call, and they will gather his elect from the four winds, from one end of heaven to the*

other. . . . Truly I tell you, this generation will not
pass away until all these things have taken place."
(Matthew 24:29–31, 34)

The kind of imagery that Jesus used in describing the End Time was part of his religious tradition and is called apocalyptic imagery. Apocalyptic imagery is cosmic. To describe the overwhelming sense of loss that people feel when their world is destroyed, authors use imagery that describes the destruction of the whole world: the sun, moon, and stars fall from the sky. We use similar imagery when we describe something that happens to us as being "earthshaking."

Apocalyptic imagery is used often in the Bible. It is used in the prophets, in the Gospels, and especially in the two books that were written in the literary form "apocalypse": the Book of Daniel and the Book of Revelation.

In fact, Jesus alluded to the Book of Daniel in his description of the Son of Man. The Book of Daniel was written for people who were facing persecution. It was meant to remind them to maintain hope, because God would send someone to free them from their political enemies. The expected messiah was described as

". . . one like a [Son of Man] coming with the
clouds of heaven. And he came to the Ancient One
[God] and was presented before him. To him was
given dominion and glory and kingship, that all
peoples, nations, and languages should serve him.
His dominion is an everlasting dominion that shall
not pass away, and his kingship is one that shall
never be destroyed."
(Daniel 7:13–14)

This messianic title, "Son of Man," is the only messianic title that is found on Jesus' lips in the synoptic Gospels. Jesus referred to himself by the title Son of Man a number of times, particularly when he warned his disciples that he would suffer and die rather than defeat the Romans (see Mark 8:31). In addition, as we have just seen, Jesus used the title Son of Man when he pictured the culmination of the coming of the kingdom and his own return.

Evidence that Jesus' contemporaries expected the Second Coming during their own lifetime is present not only in the synoptic Gospels but in Paul's First Letter to the Thessalonians. As we mentioned in chapter 1, the Thessalonians were upset because some of their number, who had become disciples of Christ and who had been awaiting Jesus' return, had died. Did this mean that they missed out on joining Christ in his final victory? Paul comforted the Thessalonians with these words:

> But we do not want you to be uninformed, brothers and sisters, about those who have died, so that you may not grieve as others do who have no hope. For since we believe that Jesus died and rose again, even so, through Jesus, God will bring with him those who have died. For this we declare to you by the word of the Lord, that we who are alive, who are left until the coming of the Lord, will by no means precede those who have died. For the Lord himself, with a cry of command, with the archangel's call and with the sound of God's trumpet, will descend from heaven, and the dead in Christ will rise first. Then we who are alive, who are left, will be caught up in the clouds together with them to meet the Lord in the air; and so we will be with the Lord forever.
>
> (4:13–18)

Paul expected to still be on the earth when Jesus returned in glory.

The Kingdom in the Gospel According to John

The fourth Gospel, the Gospel according to John, was written toward the end of the first century A.D. Jesus' spectacular return on the clouds of heaven was long overdue. John's contemporaries could easily have felt that the fortunate people were those who had been alive during Jesus' public ministry, or those who would be alive when Jesus returned. Those who were living in this in-between time were not fortunate because they were separated from Jesus.

John wrote his Gospel to try to help his contemporaries see that they were not separated from Jesus at all. Jesus had lived on the earth as a historical person. This was Jesus' first coming. Then Jesus died and rose from the dead. After his death Jesus returned, just as he promised he would. His post-Resurrection appearances were his return. The fact that Jesus rose from the dead means that Jesus is alive and is still present to his people through the Church and through what we have come to call the sacraments. John's Gospel tries to help Christians who lived at the end of the first century, and us today, to see Christ's presence in our midst. In the course of doing this, John adds to our understanding of the kingdom of God.

In order to demonstrate the truth of these statements about John's Gospel we look at a conversation that Jesus was pictured having with Nicodemus.

> Now there was a Pharisee named Nicodemus, a leader of the Jews. He came to Jesus by night and said to him, "Rabbi, we know that you are a teacher who has come from God; for no one can do these signs that you do apart from the presence of God." Jesus answered him, "Very truly, I tell you, no one can see the kingdom of God without being born from above." Nicodemus said to him, "How can anyone be born after having grown old? Can one enter a second time into the mother's womb and be born?" Jesus answered, "Very truly, I tell you, no one can enter the kingdom of God without being born of water and Spirit. What is born of the flesh is flesh, and what is born of the Spirit is spirit. Do not be astonished that I said to you, 'You must be born from above.'"
>
> (John 3:1–7)

The conversation that Jesus and Nicodemus had was about how one enters the kingdom of God. Jesus said that in order to enter the kingdom, one must be born again of water and the Spirit. In other words, in order to enter the kingdom, one must be baptized. Entrance into the kingdom does not come when one leaves the earth but when one dies and rises with Christ in Baptism. Baptism unites us with the risen Christ.

On another occasion Jesus was pictured having a conversation with a crowd who had followed him after witnessing the multiplication of the loaves. Jesus said to them,

> *"Very truly, I tell you, you are looking for me, not because you saw signs, but because you ate your fill of the loaves. Do not work for the food that perishes, but for the food that endures for eternal life, which the Son of Man will give you." . . . "I am the bread of life. Whoever comes to me will never be hungry, and whoever believes in me will never be thirsty."*
>
> (John 6:26–27, 35)

The crowd was looking for Jesus, just as John's audience was looking for Jesus. Jesus referred to himself by the title Son of Man, the title used to refer to Jesus' Second Coming. This Son of Man will give bread to eat. He himself is the bread. If we eat this bread and believe in him, we will no longer hunger and thirst for his presence. We will know that we are already in his presence. John was teaching his audience that the risen Christ is truly present to them in the Eucharist.

Later we read the story of a man born blind who received both physical sight and spiritual sight (see John 9:1–41). After the man had been cured, and as he was slowly coming to a knowledge of Jesus' true identity, Jesus asked him,

> *"Do you believe in the Son of Man?" He answered, "And who is he, sir? Tell me, so that I may believe in him." Jesus said to him, "You have seen him, and*

the one speaking with you is he." He said, "Lord, I
believe." And he worshiped him.

(9:35–38)

Again, Jesus referred to himself as the Son of Man. Jesus healed both the man's physical blindness and his spiritual blindness. The healing began with the man's being washed in the pool of Siloam, a name that means "sent"—an obvious reference to Baptism.

Through Baptism we enter the kingdom. Through the Eucharist we live in union with the risen Christ. Our spiritual blindness is healed, and we begin to see that the expected Son of Man is already present in our midst. The kingdom of God is at hand—and we, too, worship him.

In our next chapter we explore just why it is that we worship Jesus. We explore the question, Who is Jesus Christ?

For Reflection

1. Did your early religious training lead you to believe that you were earning the kingdom rather than receiving it as a gift? Do vestiges of this understanding still remain? Why is it important to your spiritual life to realize that the kingdom is a gift?

2. Do you think of the kingdom of God as a place you go when you leave the earth, or as a relationship you enter at Baptism? Explain.

3. What should we be doing to promote the coming of the kingdom of God?

CHAPTER 5

Who Is Jesus Christ?

W hen we gather at our covenant-renewal ceremony, the Mass, we stand together and express our beliefs about Jesus Christ. We say,

> We believe in one Lord, Jesus Christ, the only Son of God, eternally begotten of the Father, God from God, Light from Light, true God from true God, begotten, not made, one in Being with the Father. Through him all things were made. For us men and for our salvation he came down from heaven: by the power of the Holy Spirit he was born of the Virgin Mary, and became man. For our sake he was crucified under Pontius Pilate; he suffered, died, and was buried. On the third day he rose again in fulfillment of the Scriptures; he ascended into heaven and is seated at the right hand of the Father. He will come again in glory to judge the living and the dead, and his kingdom will have no end.

This creed, formulated in the fourth century, could never have been said by someone in the first century after Jesus' Resurrection, much less by a contemporary of Jesus. It expresses the faith of the Church in a more developed way than would have been possible so soon after Jesus' life, Passion, death, and Resurrection. None of Jesus' Apostles, during his lifetime, could ever have said, "I believe Jesus is divine." An understanding that Jesus is divine came only after the Resurrection.

Statements such as these come as a big surprise to people who presume that the Gospels are basically historical accounts written to answer the question, What happened? They will immediately claim: "Simon Peter answered, 'You are the Messiah, the Son of the living God'" (Matthew 16:16). Doesn't that show that Peter understood who Jesus was?"

The answer is, "No, that passage from Matthew's Gospel does not show that Peter understood Jesus' divinity during Jesus' lifetime." To understand why this is true, we must recall what we know about the way the Gospels came into existence. We must remember that the Gospels contain a number of different literary forms. Unless we understand the literary forms, we misunderstand the intent of the Gospel editor, and so the revelation. We must also understand the context for each Gospel, the particular conversation that was going on between the Gospel editor and his contemporary audience. Finally, we must understand the process of revelation that is revealed in Scripture, even within the canonical Gospels. All of this is to say that we need to approach the Gospels as contextualists in order to understand what they teach us about Jesus Christ.

In this chapter we, as contextualists, look at the *Christology* in each Gospel. Christology is the theological study of Jesus Christ. Christology that emphasizes Jesus' humanity is called "low Christology," or "Christology from below." It starts with the historical, human person and asks a question such as, What was Jesus' self-understanding during the time that he was on the earth? Christology that emphasizes Christ's divinity is called "high Christology," or "Christology from above." It starts with the divine person who became flesh and lived among us. High Christology asks a question such as, What is Jesus' relationship to the Father and the Spirit? As we look at the Gospels in the order in which they were written, we discover an ever fuller response to the question, Who is Jesus Christ?

Christology in the Gospel According to Mark

Mark's Gospel represents low Christology because it emphasizes the humanity of Jesus Christ. This is not to say that Mark's Gospel fails to teach the divinity of Jesus Christ. Mark's Gospel, like all of the Gospels, was written to teach a post-Resurrection understanding of Jesus: Jesus is divine. This is made clear in the very first sentence: "The beginning of the good news of Jesus Christ, the Son of God" (1:1). Mark's Gospel, however, creates a situation of dramatic irony; that is, the author and the readers of the Gospel share the knowledge that Jesus is divine as the story is told, but the characters in the story do not. Jesus' followers are pictured as struggling to come to the knowledge that the author and audience already have.

Many episodes in Mark's Gospel make this clear but none more obviously than the story of the calming of the storm (see 4:35–41). Jesus and the Apostles were in a boat during a terrible storm. The Apostles were afraid that they were going to die, so they awakened Jesus. Jesus "woke up and rebuked the wind, and said to the sea, 'Peace! Be still!' Then the wind ceased, and there was a dead calm" (4:39). When we read this, we take the fact that Jesus was able to calm the wind and the sea as an indication of his divinity. Mark intended us to understand the account that way. The possibility of Jesus' divinity, however, never entered the Apostles' minds. They were led not to a conclusion but to a question: "And they were filled with great awe and said to one another, 'Who then is this, that even the wind and the sea obey him?'" (4:41).

Not even when Peter responded to Jesus' question, "Who do you say that I am?" with the words, "You are the messiah" (8:29) did Mark picture the Apostles as understanding that Jesus was divine. Peter did not use the word *messiah* in the same way that we, in the light of the Resurrection, have come to use the word today.

Remember that Peter and all the Jews who understood covenant love expected a messiah. After all, they were living under the domination of Rome. The expectation that God would send an anointed one to save them, just as God had sent David, and even Cyrus, was always present. Peter was expressing not his faith in Jesus' divinity but his belief that Jesus had been sent by God to save them from the Romans. Jesus did not deny that he was sent by God to save. He warned Peter, however, that he was not the kind of messiah that Peter expected. Jesus told Peter, however, that "the Son of Man" (a reference to himself) would suffer and die. This was totally incomprehensible to Peter. It was completely incompatible with his understanding of a messiah. A messiah was a messiah because he defeated the enemy. If Jesus was to be defeated rather than to defeat, how could he be a messiah? It is no wonder that Jesus told his disciples not to tell anyone about him. If they did, they would spread misinformation. The Apostles would be in a position to discuss such things only after Jesus' Resurrection.

THE HUMANITY OF JESUS IN MARK

There are many ways in which Mark's Gospel emphasizes Jesus' humanity. One is that Mark did not always picture Jesus as being in control. For instance, when Mark told the story of the healing of the woman with the hemorrhage (see 5:21–35), he pictured the woman coming up behind Jesus and touching his cloak.

> *Immediately her hemorrhage stopped; and she felt in her body that she was healed of her disease. Immediately aware that power had gone forth from him, Jesus turned about in the crowd and said, "Who touched my clothes?"*
>
> (5:29–30)

Jesus' healing power seemed to have flowed through him without his taking any conscious role in the healing. Jesus wanted to know who had been healed.

Another way in which Mark emphasized Jesus' humanity is that Mark pictured Jesus as growing in his own understanding of his ministry. This occurred when Jesus met a Syrophoenician woman whose daughter had an unclean spirit (see 7:25–30). When the woman asked Jesus to heal her daughter, Jesus responded, "Let the children be fed first, for it is not fair to take the children's food and throw it to the dogs" (7:27). This response is very puzzling to us; it sounds rude. It is easier to understand, however, if we remember two things: Jesus' understanding of his own ministry and the woman's response.

Jesus evidently understood his mission to be to the house of Israel. That understanding was behind his statement to the Syrophoenician woman; she was not a member of the group to which Jesus understood himself to be sent. This understanding is actually stated in Matthew's Gospel when he pictured Jesus giving instructions to his disciples: "Go nowhere among the Gentiles, and enter no town of the Samaritans, but go rather to the lost sheep of the house of Israel" (Matthew 10:6). The fact that covenant love is offered to all is a post-Resurrection understanding (see Acts 8:5; 10:1–48). Jesus was not sure that it was right for him to give to a non-Israelite what was meant for the Israelites.

We can tell from the woman's response that she was not offended by Jesus' words. Rather than reacting as a person who felt hurt and rejected, she reacted as a person who still had hope: "Sir, even the dogs under the table eat the children's crumbs" *(7:28)*. On seeing her faith, Jesus healed the woman's daughter. It seems that Jesus expanded his idea of his own ministry in response to the unexpected events of his life.

A third way in which Mark emphasized Jesus' humanity is that Mark often pictured Jesus as being angry, sometimes unreasonably angry. During the calming of the storm, Jesus seemed annoyed. He said to the frightened Apostles, "Why are you afraid? Have you still no faith?" (4:40) When Peter remonstrated with Jesus over the idea that Jesus would suffer and die, Jesus rebuked Peter harshly: "Get behind me Satan! For you are setting your mind not on divine things but on human things" (8:33). When the disciples misunderstood Jesus' statement, "Watch out—beware of the yeast of the Pharisees and the yeast of Herod" (8:15), thinking Jesus was referring to the fact that they had forgotten to bring along any bread, Jesus appeared to be terribly angry: "Why are you talking about having no bread? Do you still not perceive or understand? Are your hearts hardened? Do you have eyes, and fail to see? Do you have ears, and fail to hear?" (8:17–18)

But the most remarkable and unreasonable expression of anger on Jesus' part appears as he and the Apostles approached Jerusalem just before his Passion and death.

> *On the following day, when they came from Bethany, he was hungry. Seeing in the distance a fig tree in leaf, he went to see whether perhaps he would find anything on it. When he came to it, he*

found nothing but leaves, for it was not the season for figs. He said to it, "May no one ever eat fruit from you again." And his disciples heard it. . . . In the morning as they passed by, they saw the fig tree withered away to its roots.

(Mark 11:12–14, 20)

This episode and the cleansing of the Temple that occurs in the same time frame (see 11:15–19) are the culmination of Jesus' anger and frustration. From this point on, even in the face of betrayal and horrible psychological, spiritual, and physical suffering, Jesus did not express anger. From this point on, Jesus seemed to accept the fact that he would die prematurely, without his disciples understanding him or what he was trying to teach them. Why did Mark give us such a human picture of Jesus?

MARK'S AUDIENCE AND MESSAGE

Mark edited his inherited oral and written accounts of the events involving Jesus about 65 A.D. Mark's audience, like Jesus, was facing persecution. The question on the mind of Mark's audience was, Why should I suffer and die? Is that what God really wants of me? By the way in which Mark edited his Gospel, by the things he chose to emphasize, Mark responded to these questions by saying, "Look at Jesus. Even though he was the divine Son of God, he was human, just as you are. He faced premature death before he had completed what he believed he had been sent to do, just as you do. He did not want to die (see Mark 13:32–42), just as you don't. Because he could not avoid death, however, and at the same time remain faithful to his Father's will, he chose fidelity over the avoidance of persecution and death. What did it lead to? Resurrection! If you choose fidelity and die with Jesus, you will also rise with Jesus."

Because Mark emphasized Jesus' humanity, if we were to ask, "When did Jesus become divine? Was he always divine?" Mark's Gospel would not provide us with a full answer. The best that we could do would be to say, "Well, Jesus was divine at least from the time of his Baptism on" (see Mark 1:9–10). We could not address the question of whether or not Jesus was divine before his Baptism because Mark's Gospel, which begins with Jesus' public ministry, remains silent on that subject.

Christology in the Gospels According to Matthew and Luke

Matthew's and Luke's Gospels are much more similar to Mark's and to each other than any of these synoptic Gospels are to John. One would expect this since Matthew and Luke both used Mark as a source. Both Matthew and Luke, however, began their Gospels in an entirely different place than did Mark. Matthew and Luke each preceded the story of Jesus' public ministry with a birth narrative. The birth narratives are christological in purpose, so a careful look at each of them helps us understand the growth in Christology that is evident in these Gospels.

When we ask Matthew's Gospel the question, When did Jesus become divine? we see that Matthew's Gospel responds to the question more fully than does Mark's. Matthew tells us that Jesus was divine at least from the moment of his conception. Matthew makes this claim by telling us the story of the angel's message to Joseph.

Joseph was engaged to Mary but, before they married, Mary was found to be with child. Joseph planned to dismiss Mary privately rather than expose her to public disgrace. But an angel appeared to Joseph and said, "Joseph, son of David, do not be afraid to take Mary as your wife, for the child conceived in her is from the Holy Spirit. She will bear a son, and you are to name him Jesus, for he will save his people from their sins" (Matthew 1:20–21). The words placed on the angel's lips express a more highly developed Christology than appears in Mark's Gospel.

The oral traditions about the significance of Jesus' Passion, death, and Resurrection developed in the opposite order from the order in which they appear in our edited Gospels. First to develop were the stories about Jesus' Passion, death, and Resurrection, because these mysterious events were most immediate in the lives of those telling the stories. Next to develop were accounts of Jesus' mighty signs. During Jesus' public ministry, the mighty signs were signs of the imminent in-breaking of the kingdom of God. After Jesus' Resurrection, the signs were understood as signs of Jesus' true identity. Who but God could have performed such mighty signs? Miracle stories were told as evidence that Jesus was divine. Next to develop were collections of Jesus' sayings. Finally, as a late development, came the birth narratives. The birth narratives are a kind of writing called *midrash*.

Midrash is a literary form that was common in Jesus' religious tradition and can be compared in terms of its function, if not its method, to a modern-day homily. Midrash does not attempt to respond to the question, What happened? Rather, midrash teaches the significance of past events in the lives of a contemporary audience. Midrash does this by incorporating biblical images into the account of events, images that cast light on the meaning of those events. As Matthew and Luke passed on traditional midrashes about Jesus' nativity, each was teaching post-Resurrection Christology for a contemporary audience.

MATTHEW'S AUDIENCE AND MESSAGE

Matthew wrote around 80 A.D. to fellow Jews who wanted to remain faithful to Judaism. Their question was, If we embrace Jesus Christ, will we be remaining faithful to our ancestors and to covenant love, or will we be turning away from our own religious traditions? Matthew responded to their question by presenting Jesus as the new Moses who has authority from God to reveal a new Law. Jesus was the fulfillment of all of God's promises to the Israelites. In embracing Jesus, they would embrace both the fulfillment of their own religious tradition and covenant love as it was newly understood in and through Jesus.

The truth of all of these statements can be seen in Matthew's birth narrative. When we read Matthew's birth narrative (see 1:18–2:22), we notice that there are some plot elements that appear only in Matthew. In addition to the annunciation to Joseph, for example, Matthew told of a star that appeared in the heavens, of magi who followed the star, of Herod's plot against Jesus, of the massacre of the children, and of the flight into Egypt. What was Matthew teaching his fellow Jews by including these unique elements in his account of Jesus' birth? Each of these plot elements recalled some person, event, or prophecy from the Old Testament. Matthew selected these particular reminders, or images, from the Old Testament because each recalled something that touched the minds and hearts of his fellow Jews. Each plot element reminded the Jews of their history, their hopes, and their sense of purpose and destiny.

For instance, the massacre of the children reminded the Jews of Moses. There was a massacre of children at the time of his birth as well. The star and the magi reminded the Jews of the prophecy in Isaiah 60.

> Arise, shine; for your light has come,
>   and the glory of the Lord has risen upon you.
> For darkness shall cover the earth,
>   and thick darkness the peoples;
>   but the Lord will arise upon you,
>   and his glory will appear over you.
> Nations shall come to your light,
>   and kings to the brightness of your dawn.
> A multitude of camels shall cover you,
>   the young camels of Midian and Ephah;
>   all those from Sheba shall come.
> They shall bring gold and frankincense,
>   and shall proclaim the praise of the Lord.
>   (60:1–3, 6)

Isaiah's prophecy was fulfilled in Jesus. The flight into Egypt reminded the Jews of an earlier Joseph's flight into Egypt, a flight that ended in the salvation of the people (see Genesis 37–47).

With every Old Testament image that Matthew wove into his account, he taught his Jewish audience that Jesus was the fulfillment of all their hopes and of all God's promises to them through the ages. Jesus was the embodiment of covenant love, and to follow Jesus was to remain faithful to God because Jesus is himself divine. Through Jesus, God had redeemed the whole human race. All of these truths were taught through Matthew's birth narrative.

LUKE'S AUDIENCE AND MESSAGE

Luke addressed a Gentile audience that lived around 85 A.D. Because Luke's audience was not facing persecution, and because they were not Jewish, the particular emphases that Mark and Matthew gave to their edited accounts were not suitable for Luke's audience. Luke wanted to emphasize the universal nature of the Good News: Jesus' saving acts were accomplished not only on behalf of the Jews but on behalf of the Gentiles as well. All people, even the most marginalized and disenfranchised, were invited into the kingdom of God. Luke, like Matthew, taught the good news of Jesus Christ's identity and saving actions not only through an account of Jesus' public ministry but through a birth narrative.

Luke also speaks of an annunciation but to Mary, not Joseph. Once more, the true significance of Jesus' birth was placed on the lips of an angel.

> *Greetings, favored one! The Lord is with you. . . .*
> *Do not be afraid, Mary, for you have found favor*
> *with God. And now, you will conceive in your*
> *womb and bear a son, and you will name him*
> *Jesus. He will be great, and will be called the Son*
> *of the Most High, and the Lord God will give to him*
> *the throne of his ancestor David. He will reign over*
> *the house of Jacob forever, and of his kingdom*
> *there will be no end. . . . The Holy Spirit will come*
> *upon you, and the power of the Most High will*
> *overshadow you; therefore the child to be born will*
> *be holy; he will be called Son of God.*
>
> (Luke 1:28, 30–33, 35)

This account contains much the same Christology that we find in the annunciation to Joseph in Matthew's Gospel. Jesus was divine at least from the moment of his conception. Instead of saying that Jesus would save his people from their sins, this account says that Jesus would establish an eternal kingdom and would reign forever.

Luke's birth narrative, like Matthew's, includes a number of plot elements unique to his account. Only in Luke do we read about Elizabeth and Zechariah, the birth of John the Baptist, the census that took Joseph and Mary to Bethlehem, Jesus wrapped in swaddling clothes and placed in the manger, the announcement of Jesus' birth to the shepherds, the presentation of Jesus in the Temple, and the story of Jesus lost and later found in the Temple when he was a young boy.

Each of these plot elements was designed to help Luke's audience come to an ever deepening understanding of the significance of Jesus' birth in their own lives. One element in particular, however, gives us an additional insight into the question, When did Jesus become divine? It is this beautiful, simple, beloved, and profound statement:

"And she gave birth to a son, her firstborn. She wrapped him in swaddling clothes, and laid him in a manger, because there was no room for them at the inn." (Luke 2:7)

In order to understand the depth of meaning in this sentence we have to unwrap the images. What would Luke's audience have understood by the word *firstborn* in relation to Jesus Christ? Remember that this story was formed after the Resurrection and after the early Church grew in its understanding of Jesus' divinity. Over time the people began to realize that Jesus Christ did not become divine at his Resurrection, his baptism, or even his conception. Jesus had existed before he was conceived in the womb of Mary by the Holy Spirit. Jesus pre-existed his life on the earth and had a cosmic role. The word used by the early Church to refer to Jesus' cosmic role was the word "*firstborn*. We see the word *firstborn* used in a high Christology hymn that appears in the Letter to the Colossians.

> He is the image of the invisible God, the first-
> born of all creation; for in him all things in heav-

en and on earth were created, things visible and invisible, whether thrones or dominions or rulers or powers—all things have been created through him and for him. He himself is before all things, and in him all things hold together. He is the head of the body, the church; he is the beginning, the firstborn from the dead, so that he might come to have first place in everything. For in him all the fullness of God was pleased to dwell, and through him God was pleased to reconcile to himself all things, whether on earth or in heaven, by making peace through the blood of his cross.

(1:15–20, emphasis added)

The date of the Letter to the Colossians is debated. While some scholars date the letter in the early 60s, others date it later. The hymn itself, however, is thought to be earlier than the letter. Scripture scholars think that the author of Colossians included in his letter a well-known liturgical hymn that celebrated the very point he was trying to emphasize to the Colossians: Jesus Christ is not in competition with other spiritual beings for supremacy. Jesus Christ is supreme, and he has brought about the salvation of the world.

This hymn, and the knowledge and faith that it contains, most likely predated Mark's Gospel (65 A.D.). Whether or not Mark knew the hymn is unknown. High Christology, however, was part of the tradition of the community at the time Mark wrote his low Christology Gospel. It is not that Mark did not know high Christology or disagreed with it. Rather, Mark emphasized one truth about Jesus Christ to meet the needs of his audience, and other Gospel editors emphasized other truths in order to meet the needs of other audiences. When we hold all the truths from each Gospel in tension with one another, we have a fuller picture of the truth.

A second letter, the Letter to the Hebrews, which dates to about 67 A.D., uses the word *firstborn* in the same way.

*Long ago God spoke to our ancestors in many
and various ways by the prophets, but in these
last days he has spoken to us by a Son, whom
he appointed heir of all things, through whom
he also created the worlds. He is the reflection of God's glory and the exact imprint of
God's very being, and he sustains all things by
his powerful word. When he had made purifi-
cation for sins, he sat down at the right hand
of the Majesty on high, having become as
much superior to angels as the name he has
inherited is more excellent than theirs. For to
which of the angels did God ever say,*

> *"You are my son;
>   today I have begotten you"?*

Or again,

> *"I will be his Father,
>   and he will be my Son"?*

*And again, when he brings the **firstborn** into
the world, he says,*

> *"Let all God's angels worship him."*
>
> (1:1–6, emphasis added)

So we see that by the time Luke wrote his Gospel, the word
firstborn had become a reference to Jesus' cosmic role. This divine
firstborn, however, was wrapped in swaddling clothes. What was
the significance of this? Again, we want to look to Scripture itself
to help us understand the full significance of the image. In the
Book of Wisdom we read the following words attributed to
Solomon:

> *I also am mortal, like everyone else
> A descendant of the first-formed child of earth;
> And in the womb of a mother I was molded into flesh,*

Within the period of ten months, compacted
with blood,
From the seed of a man and the pleasure of
marriage.
And when I was born, I began to breathe the
common air,
And fell upon the kindred earth;
My first sound was a cry, as is true of all.
I was nursed with care in swaddling cloths.
For no king has had a different beginning of existence;
There is for all one entrance into life, and one way out.

(7:1–6)

Solomon is pictured as describing himself as a human being, like every other human being. When Luke pictured the firstborn wrapped in swaddling clothes, he made a christological statement. He said that Jesus was both divine, the firstborn of all creation, and human, just like every other person.

The firstborn in swaddling clothes was laid in a manger because there was no room for him at the inn. An inn was a place where travelers passing through the area could stay for a short time. Jesus was not "passing through," however. Jesus came to dwell with his people. The prophet Jeremiah expressed the longing that God would dwell with the people.

O hope of Israel,
its savior in time of trouble,
why should you be like a stranger in the land,
like a traveler turning aside for the night?
Why should you be like someone confused,
like a mighty warrior who cannot give help?
Yet you, O Lord, are in the midst of us,
and we are called by your name;
do not forsake us!

(14:8–9)

Jesus was the fulfillment of all the longings and all the hopes of the people.

In Jesus, God not only came to dwell with the people but also became food for the people. Gospel writers probed the mystery of Jesus' eucharistic presence with God's people with various images. John, for example, pictured Jesus saying, "I am the bread of life" *(6:35)*. Luke taught exactly the same concept by placing the firstborn, wrapped in swaddling clothes, in a manger. A manger was the place where one placed the food for the flock. Jesus was placed in the manger because he was food for the flock.

A WORD OF CAUTION

Most adult Roman Catholics assume that the birth narratives are historical writing. Perhaps you, too, have assumed this. The initial effect of learning that the birth narratives are a kind of literature called *midrash* that employs biblical images to teach the significance of events is not only amazement but often resistance. When people first begin to understand that images are used to probe mystery rather than to teach facts, they experience a great sense of loss. They fear that not only is the literal understanding of an image being attacked but the truth behind that image as well. Many people, on first hearing that the images in the birth narratives are not intended to describe events as they occurred but are intended to teach the significance of those events as they were understood in the light of the Resurrection, become terribly upset. They ask, "Are you saying that all of this didn't actually happen just as it is described? Then how do we know that Christ is divine? I thought we knew Christ is divine because all these miraculous events occurred at his birth!" Instead of reaffirming Christ's divinity, as the accounts did for Matthew's and Luke's audiences, the effect of this information may be to undercut it. "Are you saying that these stories are all the figment of someone's imagination?"

Of course we are not saying that. We are saying that the early Church did not understand that Jesus was divine during his lifetime. There was certainly evidence of this, even in the Gospels that include a birth narrative. Jesus' own people were extremely resistant to the idea that there was anything special about him. When Jesus was in his hometown, the people asked, "'Where did this man get this wisdom and these deeds of power? Is not this the carpenter's son? Is not his mother called Mary? Where then did this man get all this?' And they took offense at him" (Matthew 13:55, 56). These people were certainly not aware of any star or of the kings of other nations coming to give Jesus homage. The knowledge that Jesus is divine is a post-Resurrection understanding. After the Resurrection, in the light of post-Resurrection appearances, and under the inspiration of the Holy Spirit, the early Church came to understand truths about Jesus' identity that were not understood during Jesus' public ministry. The birth narratives, late developments in the oral tradition, were told precisely to teach the Christology that was understood only after the Resurrection.

Because this sense of loss is a normal step in growing into an adult understanding of images, all those who teach Scripture should be sensitive to people who are learning this information for the first time. The birth narratives should not be taught unless there is sufficient time to teach the contextualist approach, to carefully explain the way in which images are used in midrash, and to take the time necessary to help those present integrate this new understanding into their faith life. Once the infancy narratives are correctly understood, however, their beauty, deep insights, and simplicity are overwhelming. One need only meditate on the sentence, "Mary gave birth to a son, her firstborn, wrapped him in swaddling clothes, and laid him in a manger because there was no room for them at the inn" (see Luke 2:7) to experience the truth of this claim.

Christology in the Gospel According to John

The Gospel according to John has no birth narrative. The Gospel begins with a high Christology hymn that, although it does not use the word *firstborn*, does celebrate and proclaim the truths that the word *firstborn* conveys.

In the beginning was the Word, and the Word was with God, and the Word was God. He was in the beginning with God. All things came into being through him, and without him not one thing came into being. What has come into being in him was life, and the life was the light of all people. The light shines in the darkness, and the darkness did not overcome it. . . . He was in the world, and the world came into being through him; yet the world did not know him. He came to what was his own, and his own people did not accept him. But to all who received him, who believed in his name, he gave power to become children of God, who were born, not of blood or of the will of the flesh or of the will of man, but of God. And the Word became flesh and lived among us, and we have seen his glory, the glory as of a father's only son, full of grace and truth.

(1:1–5, 10–14)

From the very first word in John's Gospel, Jesus is presented as a divine person who existed before the creation of anything else that exists. That divine person became flesh and dwelt among us.

John's Audience and Message

As we mentioned in our last chapter, John's Gospel was written toward the end of the first century A.D., to an audience that was disappointed that Jesus' expected return had not yet taken place. John tried to help his audience understand that a second coming had occurred. Jesus' birth was a first coming. Jesus had existed before his life on earth: "In the beginning was the Word." Jesus had been sent by the Father to reveal the Father's love and to redeem the human race from sin. Jesus had come again in his post-Resurrection appearances, just as he promised he would: "A little while, and you will no longer see me, and again a little while, and you will see me" (John 16:16).

After his Resurrection from the dead, Jesus commissioned his disciples to carry on his mission in the world: "As the Father has sent me, so I send you" (20:21). Thomas, however, was not present. When Jesus appeared again and Thomas was present, Jesus said, "Have you believed because you have seen me? Blessed are those who have not seen and yet have come to believe" (20:29).

The words that John placed on the lips of the risen Christ were the words that John wanted his audience to hear the risen Christ saying to them: "Blessed are those who have not seen and yet have come to believe." John wanted to help his end-of-the-century audience see the risen Christ with the eyes of faith. John wanted them to see that the risen Lord had remained in their midst and was present through the Church, and through what we have come to call the sacraments.

JOHN'S METHOD

In order to help his audience see the risen Christ, John used a completely different literary form than Mark, Matthew, or Luke used. John appeared to be talking primarily about the historical Jesus in that he told the story of Jesus' public ministry. But John was actually talking about the risen Christ in the lives of Christians. In order to accomplish his desire to tell two stories at the same time, John used allegory.

We discussed allegory in the previous chapter when we compared it to a parable. There are two levels of meaning in an allegory. The plot elements on the literal level stand for something on the implied or intentional level. The real intent of the author lies at the deeper, allegorical level. When the early Church built an allegorical sermon on the story of the sower, the allegorical interpretation made it clear that Jesus was not teaching anything about how to farm. Rather, Jesus was interested in how the seed (i.e., the Word) is received in the soil (i.e., the hearts of those who hear it).

Because John's intent was to teach about the risen Christ rather than about the historical Jesus, he presented Jesus in an entirely different way than did Mark. At every turn, John emphasized high Christology. In John's Gospel Jesus was omniscient. Jesus understood that he was divine and had come down from the Father. Jesus was pictured as saying, "I have not come on my own. But the one who sent me is true, and you do not know him. I know him, because I am from him, and he sent me" (7:28–29). And again,

> *"If I glorify myself, my glory is nothing. It is my Father who glorifies me, he of whom you say, 'He is our God,' though you do not know him. But I know him; if I would say that I do not know him, I would be a liar like you. But I do know him and I keep his word. Your ancestor Abraham rejoiced that he would see my day; he saw it and was glad. . . . Very truly, I tell you, before Abraham was, I am."*
>
> (8:54–56, 58)

John's Gospel is full of "I am" statements made by Jesus. Each of these statements is high Christology in that each is claiming that Jesus is God. "I am" is an allusion to the name that God revealed to Moses at the burning bush: "I Am who Am." Each time Jesus is pictured as making an "I am" statement, John is claiming Jesus' divinity and his oneness with God the Father.

John was not claiming that the words he attributed to Jesus in his Gospel were words that the historical Jesus said. Rather, John placed on Jesus' lips long theological sermons that explained the truths that the Church understood at the end of the first century. These long theological discourses reinforced the Christology that was taught at the intentional level of John's allegories.

We could illustrate the truths of these statements with any section of John's Gospel. We limit ourselves, however, to two examples. We illustrate that John's message was taught through allegory, reinforced by a theological discourse placed on Jesus' lips, by looking at the beginning of John's account of Jesus' public ministry. We look at the wedding at Cana and the subsequent conversation with Nicodemus. They illustrate the fact that John made the divinity of

Christ constantly visible, even as he told the story of the historical Jesus, by looking at the end of John's account of Jesus' public ministry, his account of the Passion and death.

THE WEDDING AT CANA

You are undoubtedly familiar with the story of the wedding at Cana (see John 2:1–11). Jesus, his mother, and the disciples were guests at a wedding. When the wine ran out, Mary said to Jesus, "They have no wine." Jesus responded, "Woman, what concern is that to you and to me? My hour has not yet come." Nevertheless, Jesus told the stewards to fill some empty ablution jars with water that, when consumed, was discovered to be the very best wine. The narrator's voice tells us that "Jesus did this, the first of his signs, in Cana of Galilee, and revealed his glory; and his disciples believed in him."

When authors want their audience to know that there is more to the story than meets the eye, they give their readers some signal. One signal that is sometimes used is to have some detail at the literal level of the story seem out of sync, jarring, so that we ask, Why did he say that? A jarring detail in this account is the way in which Jesus addressed his mother. Why did Jesus call Mary, "Woman?" The word *woman* reminds us of another woman who appears in the Book of Genesis, Eve. Eve was the mother of all the living. Did John intend us to make this connection?

It is true that the Gospel of John begins with an allusion to the Book of Genesis when it starts with the words, "In the beginning." Genesis begins with a story about the creation of the world. John began his Gospel with identical words to tell us not about Creation but about re-creation, about the establishment of a new spiritual order through Jesus Christ. Is the use of the word *woman* another allusion to the Book of Genesis? Should we look for a deeper meaning?

When we consider the possibility that John had two levels of meaning in his story, the evidence that our surmise is accurate falls into place quite easily. A wedding is a well-known symbol, in both the Old Testament and the New, for the relationship between God and God's people. The ablution jars stand for the old spiritual order because they represent the Law. You will remember that Jesus was often criticized for not performing the proper ablutions that the Law required. Notice that the jars were empty. This stands for the fact that the old spiritual order was no longer effective. Mary told Jesus that there was no wine. Mary stands for the Church, the mediator of the new spiritual order. Jesus called her "woman" because the Church is the mother of all the living in the new spiritual order. Jesus filled the empty jars with water that becomes wine. Water and wine are obvious symbols of Baptism and Eucharist, the sacraments of initiation into the new spiritual order.

John taught that Jesus had established a new spiritual order through the Church and through the sacraments. John wanted his audience to be able to see the risen Christ as present in the Church and in the sacraments, so that they would see Christ's glory and believe in him.

If our interpretation is correct, we will find Jesus teaching the same idea a second time through a theological discourse somewhere else in the Gospel. Soon after the wedding at Cana, Jesus is pictured as having a conversation with Nicodemus. This is the conversation to which we referred in our previous chapter when we discussed the topic "kingdom." Jesus said to Nicodemus,

> "Very truly, I tell you, no one can see the kingdom of God without being born from above." Nicodemus said to him, "How can anyone be born after having grown old? Can one enter a second time into the mother's womb and be born?" Jesus answered, "Very truly, I tell you, no one can enter the kingdom of God without being born of water and Spirit."

> (John 3:3–7)

Notice that Nicodemus is pictured as a literal thinker. He did not understand that Jesus' language was metaphorical. This gave Jesus an opportunity to explain his meaning a second time, the same idea taught allegorically in the story of the wedding at Cana: One must be born again of water and the Spirit. One must enter the new spiritual order through Baptism. By picturing Jesus as correcting the too literal thinking of Nicodemus, John nudged those in his audience who were perhaps too literal in their thinking as well. John tried to help his readers see the allegorical level of meaning in his stories.

THE PASSION NARRATIVE IN JOHN

Even as John told the story of Jesus' Passion, death, and Resurrection, he continued to keep his emphasis on high Christology. The divine person is constantly kept before our eyes. This means that John told the story very differently from Mark, who kept the human person constantly before our eyes. In John's Gospel there is no agony in the garden. Jesus did not pray to be relieved of his suffering; he was eager to complete what he had been sent to accomplish: "Am I not to drink the cup that the Father has given me?" (18:11).

In John's account, Jesus is all-knowing. The narrator's voice tells us that Jesus knew all that was to happen to him (18:4). When the soldiers approached Jesus, Jesus was completely in charge. He said to them, "'Whom are you looking for?' They answered, 'Jesus of Nazareth'. . . . When Jesus said to them, 'I am he,' they stepped back and fell to the ground" (18:4–6). As John told the story, as soon as Jesus said, "I am he," an allusion to Jesus' divinity, the soldiers fell to the ground. Jesus' divine presence was never out of sight.

John's Gospel has no Simon of Cyrene. Why would Jesus need any help? Jesus was not alone as he hung on the cross. His mother, again addressed as "woman," and "the disciple whom Jesus loved," a character who appeared only in John's Gospel, were also there. As Jesus died, he did not say, "My God, my God, why have you deserted me?" These words would have been entirely inconsistent in John's Gospel, since Jesus had already affirmed that "I am not alone because the Father is with me" (16:32). Rather, Jesus said, "It is finished" (19:30). Jesus completed what he had been sent to do. When the soldiers pierced his side, blood and water came out, once more the symbols of Baptism and Eucharist. The Church was born.

A Look Back and a Look Forward

Now that we have reviewed Christology in the Gospels, we can see that nearly everything that we say we believe about Jesus Christ when we stand together as Church and profess the Nicene Creed has a scriptural base.

The only belief professed in this creed not provided by Scripture is the answer to the question, Was Christ created, the first of all that was created? The Council of Nicea affirmed the faith of the Church by answering this question with a no. Christ is "true God from true God, begotten, not made," not a created being.

John's high Christology Gospel has prepared us for our next chapter by teaching us that the risen Christ is present in the Church and in the sacraments. In chapter 6 we explore the role of the Bible in the life of the Church.

FOR REFLECTION

1. Do you most often picture Christ as a human being or as divine? Do you know why you prefer one image to another?

2. Which of the Gospel images of Jesus do you find most compelling? Why?

3. Do you believe that the risen Christ is present now? How have you experienced Christ's presence?

CHAPTER 6

The Bible in the Life of the Church

The Second Vatican Council's document, *DV*, states that, ". . . the entire Christian religion should be nourished and ruled by sacred Scripture" (#21). Is our Catholic tradition nourished and ruled by sacred Scripture? In this chapter, we examine how Scripture nourishes and rules us in our eucharistic liturgy, our development of doctrine, our moral decision making, our communal prayer life, and our personal discernment—our desire to listen and respond to God's Word in our daily lives. We will find that Scripture has nourished and ruled us more since the Second Vatican Council than it had before the council.

Many adult Catholics would answer the question, Has Scripture nourished and ruled you over your lifetime? with a no. In fact, sad to say, many older Catholics remember being warned not to read Scripture on their own. When I was first told this, I thought the problem was isolated—some misguided individual, and not "the Church," gave this warning. I have been told by many people all over the country, however, that this was their experience as well. In fact, one gentleman brought me a copy of a page from his Bible that included the following:

> ADMONITION: . . . to guard against error, it was judged necessary to forbid the reading of the Scriptures in the vulgar languages, without the advice and permission of the pastors and spiritual guides whom God has appointed to govern his Church. . . . Nor is this due submission to the Catholic Church . . . to be understood of the ignorant and unlearned only but also of men accomplished in all kinds of learning: The ignorant fall into errors for want of knowledge, and the learned through pride and self-sufficiency.

I mention this because I think it is important for any adult educator to understand as much as possible about the life experience of those with whom we gather as we all grow in our faith together. Due to their early experience, many adult Catholics lack confidence that they will be able to correctly understand what they read in the Bible or hear proclaimed in the lectionary, even though they understand all kinds of other literature without any difficulty. As teachers, we want to rebuild their confidence as much as we possibly can. The fact that the members of the pre–Second Vatican Council Church did not experience being nourished and ruled by sacred Scripture does not mean that anyone need continue to be deprived. Now we have a clear invitation to give Scripture a core role in our spiritual lives.

Scripture in Our Eucharistic Liturgy

Scripture has a core role in our eucharistic liturgy, not only in the lectionary readings but also in the Gospel acclamation, the antiphons, the Gloria, the Lamb of God, the Our Father and, hopefully, the homily.

IN THE LECTIONARY

The Lectionary is the book that contains the biblical readings for each Sunday of the year, for weekdays, for feast days, funerals, the celebration of the sacraments, votive Masses, and special occasions. The lectionary readings for Sundays, in response to the Second Vatican Council's *Constitution on the Sacred Liturgy ([SC] Sacrosanctum Concilium)*, provide that the "treasures of the Bible are to be opened up more lavishly, so that a richer fare may be provided for the faithful at the table of God's Word" (#51).

This quotation deserves a moment of reflection. Anyone who was raised Catholic, or anyone who now worships in the Catholic tradition, is aware of the deep-seated Catholic awareness of the real presence of the risen Christ in the Eucharist. We know that when we gather around the eucharistic table, we receive the Body and Blood of Jesus Christ. By using the word *table* in relationship to God's Word, *SC* reminds us, and emphasizes, that the risen Lord is also truly present in the proclamation of the Word. "[Christ] is present in his word since it is he himself who speaks when the holy Scriptures are read in the Church" (#7). It is precisely because we believe that Christ is present in the Word that we incorporate Scripture so thoroughly into our prayer. We need to be just as attentive to Christ's presence in the Word as we are to Christ's presence in the Eucharist. How different this is from the pre–Second Vatican Council Church, in which we were taught that we had fulfilled our obligation to attend Sunday Mass if we were present from the offertory through Communion.

In those days, when we were present for the Liturgy of the Word, we heard only a prescribed set of readings from the Gospels, and a second reading, usually from the Epistles, on a one-year cycle. After the reading, a sermon was delivered, but it could be on any subject that interested the person giving it. It need not be related to the readings at all.

Since 1971, when the reforms of the Second Vatican Council were implemented, we have been dining on "richer fare." Now we have a three-year cycle that usually includes readings from the Old Testament, the Psalms, the New Testament, and the Gospels. The reading from the Gospel has the primary place because Jesus Christ is the focus of everything we do.

We read Matthew during Year A, Mark during Year B, and Luke during Year C. John is read during Lent and Easter, and on five Sundays of Year B because Mark is short. The reading from the Old Testament is chosen because it has some thematic relationship to the Gospel. The Epistle, however, is not thematically related to the Gospel. We read selections of letters in sequence in order to give us exposure to this part of Scripture.

The liturgical year begins on the first Sunday of Advent. After the four Sundays of Advent and the Christmas Season, we begin Ordinary Time, which continues until the first Sunday of Lent. Lent starts with Ash Wednesday, continues through the five Sundays of Lent and Passion, or Palm, Sunday, and ends when the celebration of the Easter Triduum (from Holy Thursday until the Easter Vigil) begins. The Easter Season begins with the Easter Vigil, lasts through the six Sundays of Easter, and ends on the seventh Sunday, the feast of Pentecost. After Pentecost, Ordinary

Time resumes and continues through the year until the feast of Christ the King, the Sunday before the first Sunday of Advent.

We see, then, that some of the time the lectionary readings are chosen to emphasize a theme (i.e., during Advent, Christmas, Lent, and the Easter Season), and sometimes the readings are chosen to enable us to become acquainted with a particular Gospel or Epistle in its own right. In either case, every Sunday is a celebration of the Lord's Resurrection. During the course of the liturgical year, we remember and celebrate all of the core truths involving Jesus Christ.

IN THE HOMILY

The function of a homily is to bring the Word that has been proclaimed from the lectionary to bear on the lives of the community gathered for worship. In other words, a homilist is not giving a homily if he decides to talk about something unrelated to the lectionary readings. On the other hand, it is not the job of a homilist to offer an adult education class on the Bible. If the homilist were to teach those gathered the literary form from which the reading came, the time in which the author lived, and what that inspired author intended to teach his contemporary audience, the homilist would not be giving a homily. Only if the homilist succeeds in putting the proclaimed Word in conversation with the lives of those gathered for worship has the homilist given a homily. The function of a homily is to bring the living Word to bear on the lives of those who hear it.

Because it is the homilist's job to interpret the readings from Scripture in a new social context—the context of the lives of his audience—the homilist is not always using a passage from Scripture to teach exactly what the original author of that passage was teaching. Homilies necessarily involve interpretation because they involve applying the core truths of Scripture to new social settings. Herein lies a possible problem. A homilist could bring Scripture to bear on contemporary situations in a way that is completely compatible with Scripture, or a homilist could bring Scripture to bear on contemporary situations in a way that is a violation of Scripture. In the second case, the homilist is using Scripture to support what he already thinks and is putting the authority of Scripture behind his own misunderstandings. An example of each will help to clarify the difference between the two.

A Valid Interpretation of a Text

On the Fourth of July, I attended a Mass at which this Gospel passage was read:

> The Pharisees went off and plotted how they might entrap [Jesus] in speech. They sent their disciples to him, with the Herodians, saying, "Teacher, we know that you are a truthful man and that you teach the way of God in accordance with the truth. And you are not concerned with anyone's opinion, for you do not regard a person's status. Tell us, then, what is your opinion: Is it lawful to pay the census tax to Caesar or not?" Knowing their malice, Jesus said, "Why are you testing me, you hypocrites? Show me the coin that pays the census tax." Then they handed him the Roman coin. He said to them, "Whose image is this and whose inscription?" They replied, "Caesar's." At that he said to them, "Then repay to Caesar what belongs to Caesar and to God what belongs to God."
>
> (Matthew 22:15–21)

Applying this reading to a gathered community of United States citizens on the Fourth of July, the homilist picked as his theme "how to be both a good Christian and a good citizen in a democracy." He discussed the choices a good Christian would make under the heading, "Repay to God what belongs to God," and the choices a good citizen would make under the heading, "Repay to Caesar what belongs to Caesar." As duties of a good citizen he mentioned paying taxes and being an informed voter, both for the common good and for love of neighbor.

But Jesus did not live in a democracy; Jesus lived in an occupied country. The Jews were under Roman rule during Jesus' public ministry. This passage from Matthew (see also Mark 12:13–17; Luke 20:20–26) obviously was not originally intended to teach the duties of a voter living in a democracy. In the original passage, Jesus did not instruct his listeners to pay their taxes. Rather, he avoided the question of taxation and spoke with purposeful ambiguity in order to avoid entrapment from his enemies.

The Pharisees were hoping that Jesus would say either, "Pay your taxes," or "Don't pay your taxes." Either way, Jesus would be in trouble. If he had said, "Pay your taxes," he would have been asking his fellow Jews to offer a graven image to Caesar, an act that was against their religion. Jews did not deal in graven images. If Jesus had said, "Don't pay your taxes," he would have been calling for a revolution against Roman authority. He would have been guilty of the charge later brought against him before Pilate: "We found this man inciting our people to revolt, opposing payment of the tribute to Caesar . . ." (Luke 23:2, The New Jerusalem Bible). Jesus slid out of the trap by replying with words that can be taken to have opposite meanings. If you were Jewish, you could understand his words to mean, "We would never offer a graven image to Caesar. That would be a form of emperor worship." If you were Roman, you could take the words to mean, "He said the Jews should pay their taxes. After all, taxes belong to Caesar." In either case, Jesus revealed the sinister motives of his adversaries. If his antagonists were the faithful Jews whom they presented themselves to be, they would not have had in their possession the coin with Caesar's image on it in the first place. The Pharisees had lost the argument in the eyes of their fellow Jews as soon as they produced the coin.

The homilist on the Fourth of July mentioned none of this. Instead he applied the sentence "Repay to Caesar what belongs to Caesar and to God what belongs to God" to the social context of his fellow worshipers. He did not use the passage to teach the same idea that Mark, Matthew, and Luke used the passage to teach.

The homilist's application nevertheless was compatible with the overall teaching of the Gospel. We should act in responsible ways for the good of our neighbor, not just for self-interest. This was a legitimate reinterpretation of the Gospel passage because the conclusion drawn is completely compatible with the overall message of the Gospel.

AN INVALID INTERPRETATION OF A TEXT

On another occasion I attended Mass on a Sunday when a capital fund-raising campaign was being launched, and the "homily" did not address the readings of the day. Rather, it amounted to a pep talk to give generously to the campaign. As part of the "homily" the "homilist" quoted this sentence from the Gospel of Luke: "So give for alms those things that are within; and see, everything will be clean for you" (Luke 11:41). The speaker went on to say (this is, believe it or not, only a slight paraphrase) that there is a connection between almsgiving and the forgiveness of sin. A substantial contribution to the capital campaign could have a positive effect on God's attitude toward our past sins. The whole presentation was reminiscent of earlier abuses in the Church and the selling of indulgences.

In Luke's Gospel, when Jesus is pictured as saying these words to the Pharisees, Jesus was not telling them that almsgiving leads to the forgiveness of sins. Rather, Jesus was warning the Pharisees that any external act, even acts prescribed by the Law, do not take the place of internal conversion. The Pharisees thought that if they gave their tithe of mint and rue, everything would be clean for them, but they were wrong. Jesus went on to say, "But woe to you Pharisees! For you tithe mint and rue and herbs of all kinds, and neglect justice and the love of God; it is these you ought to have practiced, without neglecting the others" (Luke 11:42). No amount of almsgiving would take the place of internal conversion. Only repentance and conversion lead to the forgiveness of sin.

The person who gave this "homily" abused Scripture. The conclusion he drew in applying the text to a new social setting was incompatible with what the Gospel teaches as a whole.

STRENGTHS AND WEAKNESSES IN OUR USE
OF THE LECTIONARY

The present lectionary is a great gift to the Church. If the homilist successfully fulfills his role in putting the living Word in conversation with the lives of those gathered to worship, the effect is to help us become biblical people. We begin to understand our lives, and make our decisions, in the light of the revelation that Scripture contains. We are exposed not only to those passages that appeal to us but also to passages to which we feel some resistance. These are the passages we most need to hear.

In addition, the lectionary has been a great gift from an ecumenical point of view. Because many other Christian traditions have chosen to make use of the lectionary, we are, more and more, sharing the table of the Word with our fellow Christians, although we are not yet able to share the table of the Eucharist.

The weaknesses of the lectionary are weaknesses only if we fail to read the Bible as well as the lectionary. The worship setting is presuming that we have read our Bible and that we bring with us knowledge of the biblical context of the lectionary reading. This presumption is often in error.

If we assume that knowledge of the lectionary is knowledge of the Bible, we will leave ourselves vulnerable in several ways. One is that we will have little understanding of the Old Testament in its own right. We will know next to nothing about the prophets, or even what the role of prophecy was in Old Testament times. We may well have no understanding of the uniqueness of each synoptic Gospel, despite the fact that each is read in its own cycle. Instead we may unconsciously weave the different accounts into a single narrative. As rich as the lectionary is, neither it nor the homily can take the place of our reading the Bible. The existence of the lectionary, and the necessary interpretations involved in homilies, make our reading the Bible more, not less, necessary.

Scripture in the Development
of Church Doctrine

Does Scripture nourish and rule the Church in the development of doctrine? As a Catholic, I would answer this question with a yes. Christians who are not Catholic, however, would undoubtedly be surprised by that answer. Many Christian traditions other than Catholic will not affirm any truth that is not explicitly found in Scripture. As you know, the Catholic tradition does affirm truths not explicitly stated in Scripture. Still, Scripture does rule us in our development of doctrine in that the Church, even as it interprets Scripture, "is not superior to the Word of God but is its servant" (*DV* #10). The Church cannot declare as true something that Scripture says is not true.

But Scripture also nourishes us. Nourishment helps us grow. The Church can and does declare to be true those doctrines about which Scripture contains the seeds but not the full flower and even doctrines about which Scripture remains silent. Even in this latter case, however, there must be some rootedness of the doctrine in Scripture, some trajectory apparent in Scripture from which this doctrine, under the inspiration of the Holy Spirit, has been developed.

SCRIPTURE CONTAINS THE SEEDS

In our chapter on Christology, we noted that Scripture actually teaches everything we claim to be true about Jesus Christ in our creed with one exception: Scripture does not address the question, Was the Word that existed before the creation of everything else also created? In our creed we do address that question. Christ is "begotten, not made." Our creed also contains more explicit beliefs about the relationship between the persons of the Trinity than does Scripture: We affirm that Jesus is "eternally begotten of the Father, God from God, Light from Light, true God from true God."

These creedal statements are examples of the fact that the Church, under the inspiration of the Holy Spirit, brings to fuller expression beliefs that have their roots in Scripture but that are not fully developed within the canon itself. The Church teaches what it understands to be true, both from Scripture, which is the tradition of the Jews and the first-century Church, and from later tradition, which developed in the believing community under the inspiration of the Holy Spirit.

So, for a Catholic, it is true to say that doctrine develops from both Scripture and tradition. This is not to claim, however, two sources for revelation. There is one source for revelation—the Word of God. Scripture, which is written tradition, is one expression of that revelation. Ongoing tradition is another expression of that revelation. It is the responsibility of the Church to interpret revelation. "The task of giving an authentic interpretation of the Word of God, whether in its written form or in the form of tradition, has been entrusted to the living teaching office of the Church alone . . . Yet this Magisterium is not superior to the Word of God but is its servant. It teaches only what has been handed on to it" (*DV* #10).

Because the creedal statements about Jesus and the Trinity are well developed, although not completely developed, within the canon, they have not caused division within the Body of Christ. Most Christians accept the creed as formulated in the fourth and fifth centuries. The same cannot be said for other doctrines that have their seed, but less flowering, in Scripture. A good example is the Catholic teaching on sacraments.

The term *sacrament* is not found in Scripture. There are, of course, references to actions that the Church later referred to as sacraments. Baptism and Eucharist are actions of the early Church that fit in this category. The Church, however, has gone beyond the New Testament in grouping a number of actions into one category and naming that category "sacraments."

Why some actions are included in the category of sacraments and others are not is not always clear. The development of doctrine is entirely dependent on the Spirit working in the believing community. We do consider the Anointing of the Sick, for example, to be a sacramental action. The seeds for this doctrine are in the Letter of James.

Are any among you sick? They should call for the elders of the church and have them pray over them, anointing them with oil in the name of the Lord. The prayer of faith will save the sick, and the Lord will raise them up; and anyone who has committed sins will be forgiven.

(5:14–15)

We do not, however, consider the washing of the feet to be a sacrament. This is so even though Jesus, after washing the Apostles' feet, is pictured in John's Gospel as saying,

"Do you know what I have done to you? You call me Teacher and Lord—and you are right, for that is what I am. So if I, your Lord and Teacher, have washed your feet, you also ought to wash one another's feet. For I have set you an example, that you also should do as I have done to you."

(13:12–15)

It appears that the seeds for the development of both actions as sacraments—the Anointing of the Sick and the washing of feet—are present in Scripture. Tradition, however, under the influence of the Spirit, named one a sacramental action and not the other.

Scripture Remains Silent

Even more problematic, from an ecumenical point of view, are doctrines that develop even though Scripture remains silent on the subject. As our example we pick a doctrine that is also a dogma: the Immaculate Conception of Mary.

Before we discuss this subject, it seems wise to take a few moments for some definitions. Surveys show us that the dogma of the Immaculate Conception is the most misunderstood dogma among Catholics themselves. Many Catholics think the dogma is addressing our belief that Jesus was conceived through the power of the Holy Spirit, a belief that has a fuller flowering in Scripture than does the dogma of the Immaculate Conception. The doctrine of the Immaculate Conception, however, is a teaching about *Mary's* conception, that Mary was free from sin from the moment of her conception.

This long-standing belief of the Church was declared a dogma by Pius IX in 1854. A doctrine, any official teaching of the Church, becomes a dogma if it is promulgated by the Church with its highest authority. All dogmas are, therefore, doctrines, but not all doctrines are dogmas. When the Church declared the dogma of the Immaculate Conception, was the Church being "nourished and ruled" by Scripture? As a Catholic, I would once more claim that the answer is yes. My Protestant brothers and sisters need an explanation.

Catholics believe that the Church can name as a dogma a truth about which Scripture remains silent if this belief is another step in a trajectory that is evident in Scripture. To some extent we already established this principle when we discussed Christology. If one asks, "When did Jesus become divine?" we can discover a trajectory in Scripture that pushes an understanding of Jesus' divinity back from his Resurrection, baptism, conception—even to a time before creation. The final step, that Jesus was always divine, is another step on the trajectory evident in Scripture.

Is there a trajectory about Mary within Scripture, a trajectory that sets a direction for further development in the Spirit-filled community? There is. To trace this trajectory, one need only look at the synoptic Gospels in the order in which they were written and see what each has to say about Mary.

Mark's Gospel (65 A.D.) has very little to say about Mary, and the little it says is not flattering. Mark has no infancy narrative. Mary appeared during Jesus' public ministry. When Jesus was told that his mother and brothers were outside asking for him, he replied, "'Who are my mother and my brothers?' And looking at those who sat around him, he said, 'Here are my mother and my brothers! Whoever does the will of God is my brother and sister and mother'" (3:33–35). Were Mark our only Gospel, there would never have been a teaching about the Immaculate Conception.

Matthew's Gospel (80 A.D.), while it has an infancy narrative, does not give us a full picture of Mary. In Matthew's infancy narrative, the Annunciation is to Joseph. Still, Mary's virtue is affirmed. An angel told Joseph that he should not fear to take Mary into his home because the child she had conceived had been conceived by the power of the Holy Spirit.

Other details in Matthew's Gospel seem to reflect a Church changing its mind about Mary. Matthew's genealogy mentions four women, all of whom had questionable reputations for one reason or another. Was Matthew saying that Mary was not the first woman chosen by God to accomplish God's purposes who had a questionable reputation in the eyes of her contemporaries? In Matthew's Gospel, when those in Jesus' hometown question, "Where did he get all this?" they called him "the carpenter's son" (13:55), not merely "the son of Mary," as they had said in Mark (6:4). If we had only Mark's and Matthew's Gospels, however, we still would not have a teaching about Mary's Immaculate Conception.

Not until we read Luke's Gospel do we meet Mary, the woman who was the pre-eminent disciple of Jesus because she heard the Word of God and acted on it. In Luke's Gospel the Annunciation is to Mary. The angel greeted Mary with the words, "Greetings, favored one! The Lord is with you . . . you have found favor with God" (1:28, 30). When Mary went to be with her cousin Elizabeth, Elizabeth greeted her with the words, "Blessed are you among women, and blessed is the fruit of your womb. And why has this happened to me, that the mother of my Lord comes to me?" (1:42–43). It is because of Luke's Gospel that a belief in the Immaculate Conception developed.

The three synoptic Gospels establish a definite trajectory. This trajectory reveals that interest in Mary and beliefs about Mary changed radically during the time in which the synoptic Gospels were developing. Growth in belief, along the same trajectory, continued after the canonical Gospels reached the edited form in which we now have them. A belief in the truth of the angel's words was pushed backward from the time of Jesus' conception to the time of Mary's conception. The Church grew to believe that Mary was most highly favored by the Lord not just when she conceived Jesus but from the moment of her own conception. She received at conception the grace that the rest of us receive at Baptism: She was free from sin.

Is the Catholic Church nourished and ruled by Scripture in its development of doctrine? It is. The Church cannot teach anything that Scripture says is untrue. The Church can hand on only what it receives from the Word of God, including both Scripture and tradition. Scripture nourishes the believing community that grows in its understanding of what has been revealed under the inspiration of the Holy Spirit. Scripture both nourishes and rules the development of doctrine in the Catholic Church.

Scripture in Moral Decision Making

Does Scripture nourish and rule the Church in our moral decision making? Do we, as individuals and as a community, think biblically when we have to make decisions about what actions are right and wrong? The Church in each century has had to respond to moral dilemmas that were not present in earlier generations. Have we remained faithful to the core truths of the Gospel as we have applied Gospel values to a variety of cultural settings? Have our actions been a reflection of our understanding of the truths taught in the Gospels? The fact that we use Scripture to bolster our arguments shows that we intend to be faithful to its teachings. We have a history, however, of using Scripture to support our conclusions even when we are wrong.

To use Scripture properly in moral decision making we must be contextualists. If we are not contextualists, we are not able to distinguish between the core truth that Scripture teaches, and applications or elaborations of that truth that appear within Scripture but are not part of the core truth. We may also mistake an early insight for the fullness of revelation that came later in the process of revelation. (We saw an example of this in chapter 2 when we discussed the death penalty.) Persons who are not contextualists can turn to Scripture for help in moral decision making and can inadvertently put the authority of Scripture behind their own misunderstanding. Again, an example will serve to illustrate our point.

A moral dilemma that confronted the United States was the question of slavery. If one wanted to live a life faithful to the Gospels, was it permissible to own slaves? Those who thought that it was perfectly moral to own slaves used Scripture to support their opinion. Those who thought slavery was immoral also turned to Scripture to bolster their point of view. By looking at the arguments of each side, we can gain a greater appreciation for both the role that Scripture plays in moral decision making and why it is important to be a contextualist in order to correctly apply Scripture to a different social context.

Those who thought owning slaves was a morally correct position supported their point of view by quoting the Letter to the Ephesians: "Slaves, obey your early masters with fear and trembling, in singleness of heart, as you obey Christ; not only while being watched, and in order to please them, but as slaves of Christ, doing the will of God from the heart" (6:5–6). Does this passage prove that slavery, as it was practiced in the United States, was moral? It does not.

The author of the Letter to the Ephesians was teaching a core truth: Because Christ loves each of us and sacrificed himself for each of us, we must love one another (see Ephesians 5:1–2). The author then applied this core teaching to the social structure that was present in Asia Minor at the time he wrote the letter. If his audience truly loved one another as Christ loved each of them, how would a husband and wife treat each other? How would a parent and child treat each other? How would a master and slave treat each other? The author of Ephesians never addressed the question, Is the social structure that exists in Asia Minor a good social structure? He certainly never addressed the question, Is it moral for one human being to own another? So, to use this quotation to "proof text" an answer to a question different from the question that the author of the letter was addressing is to abuse Scripture.

Those who opposed slavery could not "proof text" to show that they were right. Nevertheless, their consciences and moral sensitivities had been formed by Scripture and by the action of the Holy Spirit in their lives. When confronted with the question, Is slavery as it is practiced in the United States, where one person is the property of another for life, moral? these biblical Christians concluded that it was not. There are many core truths in Scripture that, when applied to the question of slavery, would affirm their conclusion. We can go back to the first story of Creation. That story does not address the question of slavery, but it does teach us that every human being is created in God's own image and is, therefore, of great and equal dignity. In the Gospels, Jesus taught us that the fulfillment of the Law and the prophets was to love God and our neighbor as ourselves. Is it loving to own and use another human being? The core truths of both the Old and New Testaments, when applied to a moral dilemma that came up long after the closing of the canon, lead one to conclude that slavery, as it was practiced in the United States, was immoral.

Because moral decision making involves the interpretation of Scripture and the application of Scripture to social settings different from those presumed by the authors, prayerful people of good will can disagree on various issues. It is part of the teaching role of the Church to aid and guide us in this process. The Church helps us understand the truth so that we may choose to act morally, so that our actions will build up rather than tear down the kingdom of God.

Because the need to apply the core message of Scripture to changing social settings is ongoing, the role of the Church in teaching us right actions is ongoing as well. An example of this ongoing process is present in the *CCC*. Between the time the *CCC* was originally published in French, and the time the final, official, "typical" edition was published, teachings of the pope regarding the death penalty further restricted the Church's teaching on the morality of taking another person's life as punishment for crime. These further restrictions, which were not in the French edition, are in the final, "typical" edition.

To the extent that we are faithful to the core revelation in Scripture as we apply Scripture's truths to new social settings, we are allowing Scripture to nourish and rule us in moral decision making.

Scripture in Our Communal Prayer Life

Does Scripture nourish and rule us in our communal prayer life? To a large extent, it does. All of the rites of the sacraments use biblical language. The Divine Office is structured around biblical readings.

Even the rosary, which many people think of as completely unrelated to Scripture, is heavily dependent on Scripture. The words of the prayers, for the most part, have a biblical base. The first half of the Hail Mary, for example, is derived from the angel's words to Mary in Luke's Annunciation account. The Our Father and the Glory Be are biblical prayers as well. All the joyful mysteries, all the sorrowful mysteries, and three of the glorious mysteries are based on scenes from the New Testament. Catholics are more biblical than we often realize when we gather and pray as a community.

Scripture in Personal Discernment

Scripture also nourishes and rules Catholics in their personal prayer lives and in their personal discernment to seek out and do God's will. Many Catholics have formed the habit of turning to Scripture, either by reading the daily lectionary or by reading a book of Scripture, as part of their daily prayer lives. We pass on this good habit to our candidates and catechumens in the Rite of Christian Initiation of Adults (RCIA) process when we teach them to "break open the Word." In the context of this constant conversation between our daily lives and Scripture, we have discovered that Scripture is a living word. Scripture can speak directly to each of us in the context of our personal lives, correcting us and guiding us, so that we are better able to grow in holiness.

When I first learned that many people experience Scripture in this way, I was extremely dubious. How could Scripture possibly directly address the dilemmas of an individual reader? Is such a claim, such a practice, compatible with the contextualist approach to Scripture? The answer is yes. There are cautions, however.

My resistance began to give way when I read about the experience of St. Augustine. As you may know, Augustine was not always a saint. Before his conversion, his life was incompatible with Christianity. In fact, Augustine had a mistress and a child by that mistress before he converted to Christianity. During the time when Augustine felt drawn to the Church, but before he made the decision to live his life as a Christian, he went through a painful time of discernment. During that time he heard what he took to be children chanting, "Take and read. Take and read." Augustine took a New Testament, opened it, and read: "Put on the armor of Jesus Christ and make no provisions for the desires of the flesh." Augustine understood the words to be directed at him personally, and he did as the words directed him.

My resistance entirely disappeared when I experienced Scripture as a living word in the context of my own prayer life. I was upset because someone close to me had done something that hurt me. I felt sinned against. In fact, that is exactly how I worded it to myself: "I've been sinned against." As I was reading Scripture, I read the words, "Who are you to judge the servant of another?" For some reason that I cannot explain, except to say that Scripture is a living word, that phrase seemed to correct me. As I pondered why these words should be directed at me, I realized that in thinking I had been "sinned against" I was judging another person's relationship to God, something that the Gospels constantly warn us not to do. Who was I to judge God's servant? Only God could do that. I began to "re-image" my situation. Instead of thinking that I had been sinned against, I began to realize that the other person's actions had resulted in my being hurt. I could admit and explain my hurt to the other person without judging that person's action as a sin. As you can imagine, this re-imaging opened me to reconciliation in a way that my first mode of defining my problem did not.

Experiencing Scripture as a living Word that cuts to the marrow of the bone is a common experience for people who have incorporated Scripture into their daily prayer. Is this experience compatible with all we have learned about being a contextualist? Not only are the two compatible—they need each other.

When we began our second chapter, in which we discussed the contextualist approach to Scripture, we asked whether we would think of a terrorist suicide bomber who justifies his or her actions by quoting Scripture as a religious martyr or as a murderer. It is not an exaggeration to say that many heinous crimes throughout history have been committed by zealous individuals with apparently "religious" motivations. We know from experience that such people take a quotation out of its context in Scripture, place it in the context of their own lives, hear the words as the voice of God giving them personal direction, and act on them. What is the difference between these people and me, a contextualist who believes that Scripture is a living word? I, too, take a quotation out of its context in Scripture, place it in the context of my own life, hear the words as the voice of God giving me personal direction, and act on them.

The difference is that a contextualist, before acting on the words, asks, "Is the meaning I am hearing in these out-of-context words compatible with the overall message of Scripture?" The living word, when correctly understood, will always be compatible with the overall message of Scripture. It will always call us in the direction of love.

We see, then, that just as a homilist who applies a text to a new social setting must ask, "Is the meaning I am drawing from this text compatible with Scripture as a whole?" so must an individual who applies a text to a personal setting ask this question. The living word does not always say exactly the same thing that the original author said, but neither does it contradict it. Both homilies and the living word in the context of our personal lives must be rooted in and flow from a contextualist understanding of Scripture.

It is for this reason that, as we teach our candidates and catechumens in the RCIA to break open God's Word in the context of their personal lives, we also teach them the contextualist approach to the Bible. Only when we become contextualists who have integrated Scripture into our personal prayer lives will these words from 2 Timothy be true for us:

> . . . from childhood you have known the sacred writings that are able to instruct you for salvation through faith in Christ Jesus. All Scripture is inspired by God and is useful for teaching, for reproof, for correction, and for training in righteousness, so that everyone who belongs to God may be proficient, equipped for every good work.
>
> (3:16–17)

And especially the good work of parish catechetical ministry. Let Scripture nourish and rule you in all that you do.

For Reflection

1. How does Scripture nourish and rule the Mass, the communal prayers, and the catechetical programs in your parish? What more could be done?

2. What does "think biblically" mean to you? Do you think biblically when you face a moral dilemma? Can you give an example?

3. Have you ever experienced Scripture as a living word? Explain.

Abbreviations

CCC   *Catechism of the Catholic Church*

DV   *The Dogmatic Constitution on Divine Revelation (Dei Verbum)*

RCIA   *Rite of Christian Initiation of Adults*

SC   *The Constitution on the Sacred Liturgy (Sacrosanctum Concilium)*

Bibliography

Brown, Raymond E. *An Introduction to New Testament Christology.* New York: Paulist Press, 1994.

———. *Biblical Exegesis and Church Doctrine.* New York: Paulist Press, 1985.

———, ed. *The New Jerome Biblical Commentary.* New Jersey: Prentice Hall, 1990.

Catechism of the Catholic Church. Chicago: Loyola Press, 1994.

Ralph, Margaret Nutting. *And God Said What? An Introduction to Biblical Literary Forms for Bible Lovers.* New York: Paulist Press, 1986.

———. *Plain Words About Biblical Images: Growing in our Faith Through the Scriptures.* New York: Paulist Press, 1989.

Senior, Donald, ed. *The Catholic Study Bible.* New York: Oxford University Press, 1990.

Acknowledgments

About the Author

Margaret Nutting Ralph, Ph.D., is secretary of educational ministries for the Diocese of Lexington, Kentucky. She also directs the master's degree programs for Roman Catholics at the Lexington Theological Seminary. Her doctorate from the University of Kentucky is in English Literature with a concentration in the Bible as literature. For the past thirty years she has taught Scripture to grade school, high school, college, and graduate students, and to adult education groups. Ralph is the author of eight books on Scripture published by Paulist Press.